DO YOU KNOW ANY GOOD BOYS?

Meeti is a copywriter, travel writer and a first-rate Taboo player.* When she isn't busy writing ads that make toothpaste sound like an aphrodisiac, Meeti writes personal essays and travel stories. Her work has been published in *The Wall Street Journal*, the National Geographic Society's *Glimpse*, *Jade Magazine* and *Mint Lounge*.

Meeti has dipped her feet in the Ganges, the Nile, the Bosphorus, the Amazon, the Mediterranean Sea and the Indian Ocean. She writes from a small, blue desk in Mumbai.

Do You Know Any Good Boys? is her first book.

* Her husband insists that this is not an actual employable skill, but she would like to mention it anyway.

DO YOU KNOW ANY GOOD BOYS?

A Woman's Guide to the Arranged Marriage

Meeti Shroff-Shah

PAN

First published in India 2016 by Pan
an imprint of Pan Macmillan India
a division of Macmillan Publishers India Private Limited
Pan Macmillan India, 707, Kailash Building
26 KG Marg, New Delhi – 110 001
www.panmacmillan.co.in

Pan Macmillan, 20 New Wharf Road, London N1 9RR
Basingstoke and Oxford
Associated companies throughout the world
www.panmacmillan.com

ISBN 978-93-82616-72-6

'How to Talk in an Arranged Marriage Meeting' provided by wikiHow,
a wiki building the world's largest, highest quality how-to manual.

1 3 5 7 9 8 6 4 2

Typeset by Manmohan Kumar
Printed and bound in India by Gopsons Papers Ltd

For Ma, the light of my life.
For Maulik, for showing me how to dream
big dreams.

FOREWORD

The task of finding a life partner in the traditional arranged way can be a lengthy and frustrating affair. Of course, it's not like that for everybody. I have a friend who, in a freakish instance of good fortune, married the first guy her parents set her up with and, years later, continues to remain happy. But such cases are so rare that they should be gagged and forbidden from gushing about how they 'lucked out' so that the rest of us don't land up at *our* first meetings with our wedding sarees already selected. Truth is that for most people, the process of an arranged marriage is at least as painful as delivering a pair of eight-pound twins. Without the option of an epidural.

When I agreed to let my parents help me find a life partner, I didn't think that it would be two and a half years before I'd meet the right guy. I am infinitely grateful to the powers that be for having found my husband, but the truth is, I almost didn't. I came very close to giving up, very often.

During the course of my search, I met more than forty men, and that's not counting the ones I spoke to on the phone. Some of these meetings were bland – you forgot the faces of those men as soon as you stepped out of the coffee shop. And you didn't recognize them when you bumped into them at the cinema hall a week later, and you wondered why they were staring at you so intently. Some were funny – you giggled about it with your friends until the thought of karmic repercussions diminished your enthusiasm a little. Some were infuriating – when you wrote about them in your journal, an angry impression of your words could be seen till the last page, while some were even pleasant and you became fast Facebook friends, regularly 'poking' each other – yes, I am aware of how that sounds – until things didn't quite work out and you had to block them. But they all had this in common – they led to eventual disappointment. To keep at it, month after month, Sunday after Sunday, required a patient, here-here-tell-us-all-about-it brand of support from family and friends, and an often hard-to-keep sense of humour.

These tales would've long gone into oblivion, but I often find myself in the company of successful, beautiful and single friends, who'd like more than anything to settle down, but find themselves dreading the 'arranged marriage' route. Either the idea of an arranged marriage doesn't fit in with their idea of themselves or having gone for a few disheartening coffees they are seriously considering adopting a cat instead. Whichever the case, I often find myself sharing my story with them, prodding them to keep at it and thinking that there really should be a go-to book for this sort of thing.

Do You Know Any Good Boys? is about how I finally found a suitable boy, as well as a ready guide for single, young people contemplating an arranged marriage. Starting from the day I contracted this 'mad cow disease' – what else could it have been? – and asked my parents to set me up to the time my father visited an astrologer and found that my birth chart had the dreaded 'kaal-sarp dosh' to when my Mum placed a matrimonial ad for me in the largest Gujarati newspaper and got about five and a half calls in response, it takes the reader step by step, latte by latte through the journey of my arranged marriage. Answering at the same time, questions like how to make a 'biodata', what to expect of a first meeting, how to be sure that your dearly intended is not a deranged Asaram Bapu-worshipping fanatic and why it's not okay to ask someone if they 'believe in one-night stands' – at least not in the first fifteen minutes of meeting them – all the time, urging the reader to keep perspective, to make allowances for the foibles of human nature and to hold on to that very vital sense of humour.

I DIDN'T THINK I WAS 'THAT' KIND OF GIRL

There may come a time in your life when you find yourself dancing at friends' weddings more frequently than at discotheques. Your social calendar is introduced to a new kind of Saturday night party – the bachelorette. And being a good wingwoman suddenly means helping a buddy pick a suit for his reception.

It is also around this time that your Facebook newsfeed is suddenly populated with pictures of other people's honeymoons. Friends and their shiny new spouses gallivant down your wall, sharing gelatos, clinking wine glasses, on houseboats, in hot-air balloons, on bicycles – tandem, of course, at wishing fountains, in museum queues, in infinity pools, always arm in arm, occasionally on each other's laps, and always with that same, slightly infuriating, expression on their faces – the self-satisfied smile.

It may hit you then like the waft of ammonia that escapes when someone opens the door to a train loo that, maybe, it is time to get married.

The aunty brigade – that formidable collection of middle-aged women in your life, with time on their hands and everyone's best interests in their hearts – has been trying to bring it to your attention for a while now. At weddings, those big Indian animal fairs, your mother has pushed you forward like a prized, award-winning cow, so that the aunty brigade can give your cheek a pinch, examine your fine silks and exclaim over how tall you've become.

'What are you doing these days, beta?' an aunt may ask.

'I'm a copywriter,' you say politely.

Her eyes glaze over. She doesn't comprehend what it is you actually do. You should've said freshwater marine biologist for fun, you think.

'So, you've finished studying?' she gets to the point.

'Three years ago.'

She raises her eyebrows and wiggles them at my mother. My mother smiles as if interviewing for a job.

'Do you know any good boys?' she asks.

At which point you generally walk away in a disgusted huff, leaving the older women to discuss the physical and financial attributes of young men with a frankness that only comes with age.

But you find that you've walked away one too many times. Because, lately, you've been running out of places to walk away to. Not only do your friends holiday in couples now but it seems even movie theatres, like a reincarnated modern Noah's ark, allow entry only in multiples of two. And your Facebook page, well, you'd throw something at it, if you could afford to buy another computer.

You gather your two best friends for a little heart to heart. You take stock of the men in your life. The exes, the buddies, the single colleagues and the cute salsa instructor are all scanned for potential. If you are lucky, you may stumble upon someone suitable within your own world, but sometimes, as it happened with me, you may draw a very real blank. At which point, a terrifying thought may cross your mind – the possibility of an arranged marriage.

So what gives, you ask yourself. You are a reasonably attractive girl. No double chin, no inappropriate facial hair, both earlobes approximately the same size – the guys seem to like you. A healthy dating history can attest to that. Your folks are wonderful too. They're open-minded, without a criminal record or any known mental illness, unless you count an unnatural obsession with fruit custard. But nobody knows about that. So what gives? Why isn't there a string of eligible suitors outside your door? It's not even IPL season. So where are they?

Feeling like an unhinged lamb volunteering itself for slaughter, you turn to your parents one Sunday, and just as your Dad is about to get to his favourite part in his weekly sermon – titled 'The Manifold Advantages of a Timely Marriage' – you say, to their almost comical astonishment, 'Okay.'

It is deflating. The decision to let your parents 'arrange' your marriage. With one prick, it empties you of at least half the books and movies you've consumed and almost every romantic hope you've cherished. The Darcys, the Rochesters and the Rhett Butlers of your girlhood fantasies come tumbling out, suddenly out of place in your new reality. That grand Bollywood production under way in your head where you play the lead is shelved. Permanently. And you have to make your peace with the fact that there probably is no Indian version of Tom Hanks, owner of bookstore and writer of beautiful emails, waiting for you with a red rose in a coffee shop. These dreams are no longer congruous with the future you've picked for yourself. In this future, there will be no great love story. No drama, no sweeping declarations, not even a date. Except the one they set for your wedding. Or at least, so it seems.

How do you adjust yourself to this new world view? You, with your master's degree in Literature, your colourful been-there-done-that passport and your fancy advertising job, how do you go from being 'cool' to being one of 'those' girls who has an arranged marriage?

I did it after a fair bit of kicking and screaming, and only some of it figurative. I was angry with life for keeping love from me. I took it personally. Around me, people were falling in love at work, at the gym, even at prayer meetings – can you think of a more unlikely place? Not me. I'd been out and about with a parachute, ready to leap into a relationship at the slightest change in the current, but there'd been nowhere to land. It was depressing.

In the three months it took my parents to set up a suitable first meeting, I swung from one extreme to the other – now repulsed at the prospect, now comfortable. Making myself nauseous with the yo-yoing. Until finally, I rationalized – wasn't who I spent my life with more important than how I met him?

GETTING THE WORD OUT

'You want me to add my what?!' I asked my mother, incredulously.

'Your height,' she repeated.

'Ma, come on!'

My mother and I were making my biodata. Much like the résumé you make when you're applying for a job, I was supposed to prepare an A4-sized sheet of paper with some basic information about myself, titled 'Application for Position of Bride'. Okay, I am kidding about the title, it was actually called 'Objective: To build long-term relationship in the field of matrimony; with opportunity for growth'. Okay, still kidding, but it could've been either. Seeing as I had already put down my:

Full name
Father's name
Date of birth
Educational qualifications
Current job
Past employers
References

The last one included contact information of paternal uncles, maternal uncles and anyone else your family wished to seem associated with.

And now, my mother wanted me to mention my height.

'Why not add my vital stats as well?' I asked sarcastically. So far, I'd been cooperative. Having stuck my parents with the job of finding me a husband, I'd decided to help them help me. But this was getting ridiculous.

'Don't be dramatic,' said my mother. 'Just be glad I am not asking you to put down your weight.'

'You wouldn't!' I gasped.

I was as secretive about my weight as most people are about their email passwords. Except me, the only other person in this world who knew how much I weighed was my then gym instructor, and we spoke about it sparingly, in whispers.

It wasn't like I had a weight problem. Well, there might've been a tiny one inside my head, but so many imagined and convoluted things lived there, that merely existing in my head wasn't a qualification for being taken seriously. These days, I was just considered curvy and, by general consensus, an attractive girl. But I used to be a fat kid. The kind that nobody wanted on their langdi team. My mother insisted I was just cute and chubby. But she was only being as mothers often are, blind to their children's XL-sized PE shorts. The thing is, when you've spent the formative years of your life playing Santa at the school's annual Nativity celebrations, you'll give up every national security secret before you disclose your weight. Even after you've lost seventeen kilos.

And now, here was this crazy talk of putting down my weight on a biodata to be circulated amongst extended family and friends, so that they could in turn pass it along to *their* friends. It didn't bear thinking about. I was more open to pulling my hair out with bare hands in the severe tradition of Jain monks and vowing to a life of celibacy.

I continued to glare at my mother.

'You know, I am not making this stuff up,' she said and slid an elder cousin's biodata in front of me. And sure enough, sandwiched between 'Height – 5 ft 2 in.' and 'Build – Very Slim', there it was, 'Weight – 46 kilos'.

46! Come on! Weren't we supposed to have a common gene pool or something? Life could be so unfair.

'Fine,' I said, 'but just my height.'

It was depressing how similar to a job hunt this groom hunt was turning out to be. Everything was about hard facts and figures. Birth dates, times and places were configured to draw horoscopes, affluence was deduced from zip codes and appearances from kilos, inches or whatever units of measurement had been shared. It seemed, instead of good, old-fashioned chemistry, my marriage would start with math.

But I suppose it had its uses. It was like the polite screening process of an elite preschool. You could deny admitting a toddler into your school on the basis of her admission form. If her background – the accomplishments of the toddler's mama and papa, the age up to when the toddler had been breastfed and the speed at which he had been potty trained – didn't impress you, you could say no without having to deal with the guilt of having set sight on her sweet curly head. It saved you time and it allowed you to be very picky without appearing to be so.

For instance, when my mother insisted that I mention my height, she knew fully well that I'd rather marry a lamp post than a man shorter than myself. So we put '5 ft 7 in.' in bold on my biodata to bring the cut-off mark to the attention of the aunty brigade, and to save me the trouble of owning up to some of my embarrassingly superficial criteria.

Of course, for biodatas to really work, one had to know how to read them. This came with a practised eye. It wasn't that people were dishonest, but sometimes, the facts represented weren't always in sync with, say, reality. For instance, it could be that a fond mother had tweaked a detail or two in the interest of finding her son the bride she thought he deserved. Like skipping over the education section entirely since her son wasn't a graduate and there seemed little point in drawing attention to it. Or describing a son as 'healthy', when it was clear that at 132 kilos he was definitely not going up on any gym poster, unless it was under the 'Before' section of their soft board.

Sometimes, the biodata in question was just vague. Like when it said 'Stock Market' under the head – Profession. What was that supposed to mean? Was the guy an investor in the stock market, that is, did he spend his day watching CNBC in his pyjamas, buying a 100 of Hindalco and selling some Sun Pharma on the basis of a 'solid tip' he'd received from his barber? Or was he a stockbroker in possession of the highly coveted broker's card that so many Gujarati men had wet dreams about? Or was he employed by the Bombay Stock Exchange in the capacity of an office boy? Would someone please clarify?

And then there was the other equally elusive term, the one where under Profession, they said 'Family Business'. What on earth *was* the family's business? Did they own dance bars? Hosiery shops? Did they manufacture cat food? Would it kill them to elaborate? Though some thought they *were*, in fact, being comprehensive when they wrote 'Family Business of Exports'. But what was it that they were sending out of the country? Mangoes? Little children?

'You are nitpicking,' my Mum said, 'just ask them when you meet them.'

'Yes, obviously! But why can't people take the trouble of explaining in a single line what it is that they do for a living? Surely, it's not that hard?'

Despite the fact that the hundred-thousand-sloka-long Mahabharata was written by an Indian, it is apparent that we are a country of lazy writers, and any who think to protest need only to look at their inboxes. Because waddling awkwardly around the feet of our literary giants are the great many writers of sloppy emails. Swallowing articles, spewing exclamation marks and clumsy acronyms, or disgustingly writing entirely in upper case, they invade our inboxes daily in the form of meeting minutes and briefing notes, always keen on knowing 'the status of the same'. It harrowed me that educated people couldn't string together two simple, elegant sentences. That syntax was so often slaughtered at the altar of speed. Why couldn't they just skip lunch or something if they were in such a hurry?

These days, *my* inbox had been taken over by biodatas. Some were crisp and neat, and I wanted to go meet those men and give them a quick peck on the cheek, just for having made the effort. Many, however, were vague and some even misleading – though for that, there could be another explanation. It was possible that having received a biodata for circulation, the aunties had felt compelled to recommend a few cosmetic tweaks. Like when my

5ft 2 in. friend was asked to put her height down as 5ft 4in., because after all, 'Didn't she always leave home in heels?' My friend stepped into her six-inch stilettos and took the moral high ground, but many tottered when subjected to the full blast of an aunty brigade appraisal. How else do you explain that there seemed to be absolutely no dark Gujarati men in India?

'See? No. No. And no,' I told Shilpi, my best friend, as I took her through the half-dozen biodatas my Mum had collected that month.

Under Complexion, dark men called themselves 'wheatish', wheatish men called themselves 'medium fair' and fair men were, of course, 'very fair'. There was simply no 'dark' in the shade card they all seemed to be referring to.

'It's as if all the Gujju men have become inspired by John Abraham's new beauty regimen, and have started "taking care",' I said, referring to the actor's ghastly new fairness cream commercial. 'How pathetic is it that even the men in this country are not allowed to be upfront about their skin colour?'

'That sounds so sexist,' said Shilpi.

'I know, but I am a woman, I am allowed. And anyway, that's not the point. The real problem is not that people are compelled to lie about their complexion, but that there is a "Complexion" section in the first place. You'd think that in an age where horoscopes are interpreted with sophisticated computer software, we'd have gotten over our colonial complexes.'

'I think, there is a simple solution to it all,' said Shilpi. 'If the Gujarati men just read more, they'd know that "tall, dark and handsome" was the thing to be.'

'Yeah,' I said, grinning, 'let's get all the stockbrokers and the diamond merchants a few Mills & Boon novels. That should take care of it.'

At the end of the biodata, it was acceptable to mention your Interests – like a perfunctory nod to the fact that marriage was also about the meeting of like minds and not just natal charts. This section usually escaped the radar of doting parents and the meddling aunties, and as a result, was likely to be in the same shape and spirit that it had originally been written in. It was to this section that I often turned my attention and much to my parents' dismay, based my decisions on the men I would or would not meet on the items I found there.

For instance, 'Watching TV' was generally a no go. Don't get me wrong, I put in a solid hour of loving *Raymond* every day. But that wasn't a hobby. A hobby is 'an activity pursued outside one's regular occupation and engaged in primarily for pleasure' and vegetating on the couch, regardless of how pleasurable it was, wasn't an active pursuit of anything. But I was always willing to overlook 'Watching TV' if it was preceded by something cool, like playing the ukulele or snowboarding or Scrabble. I realize that this is probably the first time in the history of the English language that the words 'Scrabble' and 'cool' appear in the same sentence, but in my world, Scrabble was up there, alongside world travel, highbrow literature and the 'Sunday Style' section of *The New York Times*. It was also way above things like that most unoriginal of interests amongst Indian men – cricket.

There was just no escaping cricket. It was on every list. Even the guys who wore original Messi T-shirts during the FIFA World Cup and stayed up all night to catch the game and brag about it the next day, acknowledged it as their first love. It was like a secret bro code for Indian men: *Whether or not a bro cares about cricket, a bro cares about cricket.*

Commonplace as it was, cricket was acceptable. I suppose high-fiving your buddy while using the other hand to push the volume button on the remote, grab a pack of chips and scratch your balls at the same time could pass off as an active pursuit. And if Sehwag was in form, there was certainly some amount of pleasure to be derived from it.

But what of the men who listed 'Surfing the Internet' as their hobby? Seriously, what *was* that supposed to mean? We are children of the twenty-first century. The World Wide Web is our playground. I get it. But surely, watching 'Gangam Style' on YouTube a zillion times a day doesn't qualify? Or are we talking about 'Like'-ing kitten videos and throwing sheep at each other on Facebook? Or is it that guy thing – compulsively loitering on the Apple homepage to drool over the latest iPhone in the market? Or am I coming at this completely wrong? Is the Internet actually a euphemism for surfing porn? It would be great to know what we are talking about here. Because the last I checked, googling isn't like golfing or gardening. It says absolutely nothing about you, except that you have occasional access to a computer with a connection to the Internet.

In the interest of saving everyone involved a whole lot of time, biodatas have, of late, started being accompanied by pictures. At first, the thought of my photograph floating about strange living rooms and being handled by grubby – I have no idea why, but that's how I imagined them – fingers was disturbing. But when I had sat through a few meetings, one of them with a delicate flower of a boy who couldn't have weighed more than thirty-five kilos, wishing ardently that it would've been nice to get a little heads-up, I quickly came around, agreeing to send a picture in return for receiving one. Because compared to biodatas, which were reticent when it came to divulging anything useful, a picture practically prattled.

The picture you received was usually a slight variation of one of these:

1. Guy in a suit, against a dirty, bright red or blue curtain – that trademark of the Indian photo studio – smiling into the camera with hands inside his trouser pockets. *What you took out of it:* Look I actually took the trouble

of wearing a suit and going to a studio for this picture – that's how badly I want to get married. Also, please note how comfortable I am in my suit. It not only shows that I wear suits on a regular basis, but also that I frequent the sort of places where suits are required – namely, the annually occurring wedding receptions of my many cousins in Bhavnagar, Gujarat, which gets very cold during the wedding season.

2. Outdoors. With one thumb hooked in the belt loop of a pair of denims and one leg raised smartly on a step, often with a cap.
   What you took out of it: I am an active, sporty kind of guy. Don't be fooled by this little jiggling fold of fat hanging over my belt. It's from all the beer I consume when I go to the sports bar to watch sports with my buddies. And don't miss my Manchester United cap. I don't wear it because of my receding hairline, I wear it because I love sports. Jeez!
3. Guy with arms wrapped around grandmother or some such appropriate family member.
   What you took out of it: I am a warm, family-loving kind of guy. In fact, I am so fond of my family that try as I might, I couldn't find a photograph of myself without them in it too. Also, I have watched *Hum Saath Saath Hai* 118 times.

Okay, so maybe I am not being completely fair. In the interest of my fast depleting karmic currency –

what, you think we can go on making snide comments about innocent people without any repercussions? – I should admit that not all of them were as lame as that. Sometimes, despite the paunches and the unfortunate choice of clothes, there would be a redeeming pair of kind eyes or a smile that was as cheering as the sight of an old friend and I'd gladly go to meet those guys. In fact, I was even willing to overlook things like 'going for a drive' in the Interests section or 'senior executive for MNC' in the Profession section and all sorts of other minor outrages in the biodata, if the guy in question had an open, intelligent face. Though I couldn't help but be tickled when we received not one, not two, but all three of these pictures from one guy. What was this? Gladrags Manhunt 2008? Or had the guy just not been able to pick his best? Or perhaps it was his mother who had sent them, because that would explain so much.

4. Even though I giggled about the three-picture guys, I'd pick them any day over the guys who sent the fourth kind of picture. All I can say about them is, 'Huh?' Very often – yes, amazingly, it happened with some regularity – a guy would send just one distant photograph of himself, invariably in front of the Eiffel Tower or some such iconic foreign attraction, and express regret at the lack of clarity.

My point was: *Are you kidding me?* I can't tell whether you have a nose in this picture, let alone any hair, so what am I to gauge? Your general aura? It is commendable that you've set foot outside the country and Paris, no less. But this is not a Yash Chopra movie. The exotic, foreign backdrop is not the star attraction, you are.

MY FIRST TIME AND MY SECOND 'FIRST' TIME

A first arranged meeting is exactly like your very first gynaecologist appointment. Awkward as hell. You begin to dread it the moment it is set up. The closer the date approaches, the more frantic you get, until at the designated hour, you find yourself sitting across a strange man asking and answering some very intimate questions. Sometimes if you are lucky, the doctor has good bedside manners, in which case he may make small talk and crack a few jokes so that it is all a little less embarrassing. But friendly or not, when you come back from that first arranged meeting you are likely to feel as vulnerable as if you've just had somebody tinkering around your private parts. In retrospect, perhaps the only difference is that instead of being handed a paisley-print hospital gown in exchange for your pants and a bit of your dignity, you get to wear something pretty. That, and the fact that there may also be an audience. In the arranged marriage scenario, it is common for parents and even extended members of the family to be privy to the proceedings. As if the meeting itself is not humiliating enough, it must also be deconstructed during the car ride back home.

I didn't sleep much the night before my first meeting. Mainly because I couldn't believe I had actually agreed to marry without love. So far, my decision had had that unrealness one usually associates with freak tragedies that happen to other people. I didn't really think the Universe would make me go through with it. A part of me – the one that collected clippings of the 'Love is' column from the *Bombay Times* to stick into a scrapbook – had believed that this was just the final test of endurance in my quest for true love. Like in the movies, when things got really crappy for the heroine, before they got better. But here I was with a thick paste of curd and honey on my face, so that I'd be all smooth and radiant for my 'date' the next day.

The only remarkable thing about my first meeting was that the guy's name sounded a lot like mine. Can you imagine a wedding card that read 'Meeti weds Mitesh'? We'd have had to say 'No flowers, gifts *or* jokes please'. Other than that, the entire evening had the air of a bad theatre production. Think one of those new-age plays where they are trying to keep things so real that absolutely nothing happens. There was no memorable dialogue, no climax and no character who stood out. What we did have was a clichéd script and everyone stuck to it. The parents discussed *Kaun Banega Crorepati*, the hero focused on memorizing the menu and the heroine sent desperate text messages to her best friends, telling them that this was the most embarrassing, horrid, insipidly boring thing she'd ever done.

I came back from the meeting so gloomy that I'd have fit in a movie Anurag Kashyap might've directed while on depressants. And my parents, as if they'd had an out-of-body experience and had not really been present the whole time, were already discussing the next person they wanted to set me up with during the car ride back home.

'Are you guys deranged?' I had asked them. 'Do you really think I'd put myself through that again?'

But I did. I had more than forty 'first' meetings. Each time propelled by the thought that maybe next time would be different. Next time, perhaps, I'd meet a man who would make me laugh.

From experience, here are the different kinds of first meetings it is possible to have.

GIRL MEETS BOY

This kind of meeting is ideal. In fact, it is pretty similar to a blind date – the guy and the girl may talk on the phone or exchange messages and fix a time, day and place for their first meeting. However, on an actual blind date, the chances of your date turning out to be a gorgeous mass murderer are high, because of which the evening has an air of delicious anticipation. In an arranged meeting, the background of the 'date' has been so thoroughly vetted that he already has the blessings of your parents and is, as a result, infinitely less exciting.

Also, unlike in an actual blind date where you can choose from any number of mutually appealing activities like catching up for a drink, a dinner and a movie, or go-karting, in an arranged set-up there is usually one kind of 'date' you're advised to go on – coffee. Regardless of the fact that you may actually be meeting at lunchtime. I suppose one reason is that a coffee is flexible – depending on what you think of your date, you can either make it a quick coffee, a lingering coffee or even two coffees. Imagine if you met someone for dinner and didn't like them from the moment they said hello – it's possible, some people have very shifty eyes – how would you last through dessert? Having a friend call you pretending she has a flat tyre only ever works in the movies, you know. Nobody's really going to buy that you know what a car jack is, much less how to use one – which might have been offensive, if only it weren't true.

A coffee, on the other hand, lends itself well to quick exits. A small latte, usually, takes about six minutes to come and ten to finish – What do you want me to say? Yes, I timed it. He was a nice person who manufactured plastic plug points or something that sounded like that. I was bored out of my mind. So basically, you're good to go in twenty, unless, of course, the other person has ordered an Oreo-flavoured mocha with two scoops of vanilla ice cream. In which case, you are more or less stuck. You could fake a seizure and throw yourself on the floor, if you are really desperate for an exit. But you may be sure that word of it will eventually get around to the aunties and you really don't want *them* asking questions.

The other good thing about meeting for a coffee is that it is more routine, more everyday. You are relaxed at a coffee shop. Nice restaurants, on the other hand, are intimidating by design. You can't help but be conscious of your hushed surroundings. You worry about ordering the right item on the menu – it can't be too messy, it can't be too pricey and heaven forbid if you don't pronounce it right. With coffee shops, you know what you want before you even get there. Saying 'cappuccino' is about as complicated as it gets. The person in front of you can have your complete attention.

I suppose the same argument could be made about meeting at a bar – the setting is casual and you already know you enjoy martinis, ergo, you are free to focus on the conversation. In fact, I suspect that the alcohol would even calm those nerves and help move things along rather nicely. Add to that some Simon and Garfunkel and mood lighting and the two of you might actually convince yourself that this has the makings of a romance. Seriously, if they started having arranged meetings at bars, kids would be asking parents to set them up all the time. Hell, arranged marriages would even acquire a slight modicum of coolness. What? You don't think so? Not even then? Fine. But at the very least, we arranged-marriage people would be able to hold our own against the perennially inquisitive, love-marriage people who're always asking, 'So where did the two of you meet?' *Why do they even care?* 'We met at a bar, pretty face. Now beat that.' If only we could say that, it would do the arranged-marriage system such a world of good.

But I don't have the kind of courage required to make that suggestion to Hansaben and Jyotsnaben, the two stalwarts of the aunty brigade who run a popular matrimonial bureau in our part of town – not even in this book, not even after having been married six years. After all, I have a younger brother who may yet need their services.

Coming back to being comfortable in coffee shops, I once met a chartered accountant who refused to be drawn into conversation the entire time that we had our coffee.

'So how do you spend your Saturdays?' I asked him at one point.

'I go on long drives, listen to music,' he said, before resuming his staring contest with the coffee cup.

'That sounds like fun,' I said and checked my phone for the hundredth time. No messages or calls. Where were the Vodafone guys and the Mahindra Holidays executives when you actually wanted to hear from them?

'So what kind of music?'

'Mostly old ghazals ... some Kishore Kumar.'

'Nice...'

He shifted in his seat again and I went back to looking out of the window, which fortunately, faced the road and offered some distraction. I had finished my coffee and was almost at the fag end of my usual repertoire of conversation topics, but he was just halfway through his. I mean the coffee. I am pretty certain he didn't have a repertoire of anything.

I volunteered, 'I like to watch films and ... I love to read.'

'Nice.'

'It is.'

Silence.

He shifted in his seat again and took another small sip of the coffee. I sighed and began to think of all the stores I had to visit that afternoon. It was July, the official sale season in Mumbai. All the shop windows were decked in crimson, the colour that warms the very cockles of a true shopper's heart. There were great deals to be had on Aldo, Mango, Promod, basically on all of the overpriced international brands, which, as a self-respecting Gujarati woman, you didn't allow yourself to even glance at during the non-sale months. But to make the most of the season, you had to approach your shopping with strategic cunning. For instance, there were women who left their breakfasts halfway and rushed to the mall the very day Zara released its full-page sale ad in the *Bombay Times*. Their naivety – and I am being polite here – had always amazed me. Because, as everyone – probably even the guy who sold chaat outside the mall – knew, the brands always began the sale with minimal 10 or 20 per cent markdowns and only deepened the discounts as the season progressed. Secondly, they rotated the stock across their different stores in the city, so that every other week there was something new at *your* mall. Which essentially meant that you couldn't max out your credit card on day one. To begin with, you made a note of the things that caught your eye. Then, unless you were so enamoured by something that you couldn't imagine a meaningful existence without it – happens to the best of us, no shame in it – you just let everything be. You stayed close and you kept watch. Eventually, from 'Up to 50%', things would be marked as 'Flat 50%'. And that is when you swooped in to make your first big purchase. That's right, this was only your first. Because, as any veteran shopper knows, what falls to 50 per cent rarely stops there. Seventy per cent was your sweet spot. When you shopped at '70% off', you knew you had beaten the house – yes, even when you ended up buying things you didn't really need, jeez, who are you? A man?

Sure, this approach required multiple visits to the mall,

but if you compared it to the prodigious amounts of time the early birds spent languishing in queues outside the changing rooms, it probably added up to the same thing.

Seeing how pressed for time I was, you can imagine my relief when the chartered accountant finally finished his coffee and enquired whether he could ask for the bill. I nodded so vehemently that I almost hurt my neck. Then, just as we were walking out, he asked, 'Are you going home?'

'Yes.'

And then to my horror, he said, 'Why don't I drop you? You are on my way.'

I could think of very many reasons for why he needn't have bothered – the least of all being that at this point, shutting my eyes and gently twirling an ear bud in my ear seemed infinitely more stimulating than his company. But always terrible at coming up with a good spontaneous excuse, I said, 'That'd be great.'

When we got into the car, a Maruti Zen, something strange happened. 'So what do you think of the Amul hoardings?' he asked, as he adjusted the rear-view mirror. 'And what about the new Shah Rukh movie? I think Farah Khan is a great director. Do you like Hindi movies?'

It was as if the key in the ignition had not only kick-started the engine, but also that part of his brain that controlled the ability to conduct speech. He held forth on the dismal state of Indian cinema, and how he loved cars and the Mumbai monsoons and so on, right until we reached my building, when he asked, very hopefully, 'Would you like to go on a longer drive?'

I really didn't. It was great that he was finally talking but I didn't see a future with anyone who needed to get behind a wheel and strap on a seat belt just to be able to talk to a girl. But before I could politely demur, we'd already passed my house. I resigned myself to the drive. Jagjit Singh was belting out something heart-wrenching and lovely on the car stereo. I'd live. Surprisingly, he kept up a constant stream of chatter until we'd driven for half an hour and were in sight of my building again. Here, he looked at me expectantly and asked, 'Shall we continue?'

This time, I had my excuses ready and I promptly declined. The morning, however, was an interesting study on comfort zones, or as my friends took to calling it, *comfort zen*.

GIRL MEETS BOY – WITH CHAPERONES

'Is someone going to ask me how I feel about all this?' I asked my mother, who'd just concluded a phone conversation where she'd set up a meeting for us with a guy and his parents.

'I did ask you. And you said you didn't mind meeting him,' my Mum said, being obtuse on purpose.

'Yes, "him". I wanted to meet him. Nobody said anything about two sets of parents tagging along.'

My Mum gave me one of her looks that said, come on, how many times are we going to do this?

'Isn't it bad enough that you guys are setting this up? Do you have to sit in and take minutes of the meeting too?'

'Beta, you know it's not up to us.'

I knew it wasn't her idea but it was an upsetting state of affairs all the same.

An arranged marriage, it is often said, is not only the coming together of two individuals, but also two families. Which essentially meant that when you agreed to an arranged marriage, you made your love life the very legit business of your parents. Suddenly, nothing was off limits. Not only were you expected to discuss your evening with them when you returned from a date, but they also thought nothing of actually accompanying you on one.

I didn't like the parents to come along. Without them there, the meeting had at least the semblance of a date. If you were having an interesting enough conversation with someone, you could momentarily, never more than that though, forget how you'd met them. But with the parents watching, you felt like you were under investigation. You arrived at the police station, your lawyers in tow. Eventually, one of the cops took you aside for interrogation, while the rest sipped on bad coffee and observed you for facial tics through a two-way mirror. It was truly the third degree.

At my age, my Mum was running a small business, managing her home *and* dealing with an ill-tempered, colicky baby. Surely, I was old enough to decide if a guy was interesting enough to meet a second time? My parents were willing to grant me that. But often, after the biodatas had been exchanged, when it came to arranging a meeting, the guy's parents informed us that they'd be accompanying their son, leaving my parents no choice but to follow suit.

'You know, there is an upside to us coming along. A conversation with the parents can tell you something about the kind of children they may have raised,' said my Mum, who believed that children had a lot of their parents in them.

Now I have friends who are so unlike their parents that they might as well have been found bawling in a basket on the steps of a hospital. But I was growing up to be a lot like Mum. Right from my acute distrust of allopathy and chronic impatience with latecomers to my outrageous sweet tooth, a lot of it was inherited. I could see her point.

Besides, there was a sort of unwritten cap on the number of meetings you could have with the same person. For instance, where I came from, you couldn't meet more than five or six times without expressing serious intent, and in some conservative cultures even that was considered a bit much. This 'curb' made a first arranged meeting, more than anything else, a data mining exercise. You gathered all you could about the opposite side in the duration of that first coffee. From the car they arrived in and the clothes they wore to what their accents said about the schools they'd gone to, everything was noted and filed away for future analysis. Which was also why parents insisted on sitting in on meetings, so that while the children talked, they could get a head start on the field research. It was all very reasonable if you were looking at it as an objective bystander but from the point of view of the main concerned party, that is me, it was an extremely depressing way of finding your life partner.

Picture this: you walk into a coffee shop with your parents for your coffee date with the guy and his parents. Everybody smiles and invariably arranges themselves around the table, so that the fathers and mothers are exactly opposite each other and you're opposite your date. One of the parents begins the small talk, which for some reason always starts off with who we all know in common. The Gujaratis are a large but surprisingly well-knit community, and it turns out that we usually know someone they know, an ex-neighbour, the local physiotherapist, a favourite paan-wallah – no matter how tenuous the connection, once it is arrived upon, it is grabbed with gusto and squeezed and milked like a pair of cow's teats. While the parents are thus playing Farmville, the two young people alternate between scanning the menu and surreptitiously checking each other out. At one point, somewhere in the pause between the enumeration of Narendra Modi's many fine qualities and the vagaries of the Indian stock market, the mothers give their respective children a little nod.

This is usually the signal for us, the two people on the date, to shift to a separate table – and actually begin our date. It always surprises me that the waiters don't seem in the least bit curious about this behaviour. They lead us to an appropriate table, one that is within sight of the parents but out of their earshot, without ever mixing up our orders, all very matter of fact. Once alone, the guy and I chat about this and that. Usually ticking off a set of questions, unless the conversation digresses naturally which is always a pleasant surprise. When our drinks are over, we head back to the main table, feeling a little like explorers heading back to the mother ship.

Now, I realize that this should've been impossible to say with a straight face, seeing as an arranged marriage was the most perfect antithesis there was of a space expedition. But it seemed to me that it required a certain kind of bravery and a leap of faith to stake your life in a marriage that was the result of four chaperoned coffees. For the sake of my sanity, it was important that I think of the process as an adventure, something out of which I'd get at least a life experience, if not a life partner, because otherwise, without the right perspective, trying to find love on this orchestrated, much monitored, non-date was potentially soul-crushing.

Every now and then though, even I was forced to concede that it was a good thing the parents had come along. For instance, once I was meeting a guy, a consultant at one of the Big 4, at a coffee shop. So far, he had asked all the right questions and even cracked a few jokes. We'd had an easy conversation at a separate table before joining our parents back at the main one. I'd have gone so far as to say it was going well, until the guy's father announced, 'We just bought a 2,000 sq ft. apartment.'

'That's nice,' my father said.

'In Santacruz.' He paused for effect. 'West.'

Now, for those unfamiliar with Mumbai's geographical dynamics, Mumbai is divided into 'town' and suburbs, and the western side of any suburb is usually the more expensive part of the city. It was a matter of pride for the denizens of suburbia to add 'W' to their addresses. It was considered more elite and affluent – by everybody except those who lived in south Mumbai, or town, as it was referred to by locals, and who didn't spend a whole lot of time considering the suburbs in the first place.

My parents, 'townies' through and through, smiled politely.

'We've hired an interior designer,' he continued, then turning to his wife, 'did you tell them our son just got promoted?'

His wife shook her head, the son had the decency to seem embarrassed, but not enough to tell his father to change the subject. He excused himself to go to the restroom, while his father continued in the same vein.

'Kaushal will bring home a package of twenty-eight lakh this year. And that's over and above his stock market investments,' he said, looking around the table expectantly, as if he'd just served up a magnificent tandoori chicken and was waiting for everyone to tell him what a fine job he'd done. The waiter had just come with the bill, and my father chose that moment to count the money and make the payment. I, as I was expected to, continued to study my toes and fiddle with my phone underneath the table. Which left my mother to come up with a suitable response, but before she could say something, the guy's father looked straight at her and asked, 'So, how much did Meeti make last year?'

The question was in such spectacular bad taste that I was glad it had been raised. It made things very easy. This was not a family I wanted to be part of, and now there was no need to give them the benefit of doubt. My enthusiastic parents, in their zest to see me married, would've made allowances for their 'interior-decorated house'. 'They were trying to make a good first impression,' they'd have said to mollify me. However, this crude tossing about of numbers hadn't gone down well with them either. And I could see from the slight flare of my mother's nostrils that she was about to speak her mind. But the son returned just then, and my father took the opportunity to push his chair back and ask politely, 'Shall we?'

After that meeting, I complained a little less about parents accompanying their sons. I knew it was unfair for children to pay the price for their parents' foibles. I was reminded of how Darcy wrote off his love for Elizabeth because her family was silly and vulgar, only to realize later how unlike them she was. But the rules that apply to great literature, as I was painfully learning, could not always be applied to life. The stakes were just too high.

GIRL MEETS BOY – WITH INTERACTIVE AUDIENCE

This sort of meeting was just sprung upon you. You went there expecting to meet the guy and his parents and instead, met more than half a dozen family members gathered around the table like it was young Himesh's birthday party. I have always been curious about this sort of a meeting. Why were these people there? Was this some kind of family outing? Did they think they'd come for a Sunday matinee show? Did they tell themselves, let's go see a girl today? Or were they part of the core advisory committee? The 'Let's-help-young-Himesh-decide-whether-he-should-meet-the-girl-a-second-time' panel? Because really, the only thing a first meeting was going to lead up to was a second meeting, so why the fuss? I know that marriage is a big decision, and that two heads are often better than one, but was the guy really going to defer to his iced-tea slurping, Justin-Bieber-T-shirt-sporting, eighteen-year-old sister on whether I was potential life partner material? Sure, lovers of Justin Bieber can be discerning – come, let's not be mean – but even they need something to go on.

Her: Hi, cool top.

Me: Thanks.

Me: What college do you go to?

Her: HR. But I hardly ever go.

Our little exchange, punctuated by long slurping sounds, was hardly going to be the deal changer. So what was her role here? Or for that matter of the various uncles, aunts and third cousins who routinely made special appearances at such meetings? For the most part they just sat there, checking me out from time to time and making astute little observations like how hot Mumbai was getting with every passing summer.

I've only had one meeting where it was imperative that the extended family be there – seeing as the son wouldn't be talking at all. As usual, once we'd served our time at the main table, the guy, a shy diamond trader, and I rose to go to our separate table. To my surprise, the guy's sister and brother-in-law followed suit. This was to be the start of the 'date' part of our evening. Here, in the course of getting to know each other better, I could confess about wanting to get a tattoo and he of his addiction to Coke – the Coca-Cola variety of course, we are Gujaratis and the only drugs we can't do without are antacids – without anyone taking down notes.

We'd just settled around our table, much like two couples on a double date, when the guy's brother-in-law asked, 'So Meeti, do you cook?'

I wanted to say, 'Not really, do you?' but it would've been considered rude. Although I am not entirely sure why since I would just be asking him what he had asked me. In the same vein as 'So Meeti, do you ski?' 'Not really, do you?' But I just smiled and said, 'Sometimes.'

'Do you enjoy it?'

'Uh ... yeah, it's not bad.'

'Our Bhavtik, here, is a great foodie.'

Bhavtik blushed and began to read the future in the dregs of his empty teacup.

'Idlis and medu vadas are his favourites. So what dishes do you make?'

'Pasta.'

'How about nice round rotis?'

If I were a little kid, this could be the moment I flung a toy car at his face. But I was a grown woman looking to get married, the most I could do was finger the sharp edges of my fork under the table and consider stabbing his eye. What was with him and food anyway? Had he not gotten any breakfast that day? Or had he been watching a lot of *Khana Khazana* lately? Or was he just looking out for the interests of Bhavtik and any future children we may have together? 'Can this woman stir the fires of the hearth?' Is that what we'd have heard if this were a saas-bahu soap and all the characters' private thoughts were made to resound loudly while the camera zoomed in on their conspiring faces? Because, and even though I was no bra-burning feminist, this line of inquiry was really beginning to annoy me. In fact, the most critical question in the scheme of things was – why was he talking at all? As far as I could tell, he already had a woman to stir his fires.

I looked at the man's wife and almost gave her a pitying smile, nobody should have to put up with this every day. Then I assured him that I hadn't made a single roti in my life, and unfortunately, not even vadas.

GIRL MEETS BOY – WITHOUT THE BOY

Sometimes, the guy in question worked abroad and was going to be in town for just a few short weeks. In that time, he'd have to meet as many girls as his parents could possibly line up and pray that one of them turned out to be the *one* – if this plan didn't work, he'd have to go back, collect more leave, while his parents collected new biodatas, and return to India in about six months to try his luck again. Because of the Bingo-like nature of this method, the parents of these guys were always a little more frantic. They wanted to 'shortlist' the girls their son would meet on his short two-week trip by first meeting the girls and their parents themselves. It goes without saying that the only other gathering duller than this sort of meeting was a seminar on tunnel boring machines. And there, at least, you wouldn't be judged if you nodded off and a little drool trickled down your chin. Because when you and your folks met up the guy's parents without the guy, everybody's centre of attention became you. You were exactly like a conversation piece in someone's drawing room. Much like guests admiring an exotic blue and yellow parakeet, the parents of the guy would look at me appreciatively – I hope – and ask my parents questions about my schooling or work. And my parents would answer enthusiastically, as if they were indeed describing their trip to the Amazon where they had chanced upon the parakeet and not their only daughter. From time to time, I would be expected to answer a question all by myself and all four pairs of eyes would converge on me as if the parakeet had learnt a funny new phrase and had been asked to repeat it for the benefit of the guests. They'd all smile at me when I had finished, regardless of what I had said, and go back to discussing the Amazon. It was so excruciating that I put an end to these kind of meetings after a guy's mother made my mother and me wait in a coffee shop for forty-five minutes and then bustled in with questions about the parakeet, without so much as an apology.

In retrospect, these dates may seem funny but at the time there wasn't anything sadder in the world than coming back home from yet another first meeting that would never lead to a second. Sometimes I think, I hurt more for the sake of my parents than my own. They weren't shielded by the buoyant arrogance of youth that often screened me. Disappointed after yet another unsuccessful meeting, I'd concoct defiant fantasies about living alone in a big European city and studying creative writing at a lakeside workshop. I didn't *need* to be with someone to be happy – it'd be nice, sure, but if it wasn't meant to be I could nevertheless imagine a glorious future where I travelled the world on book signing tours. Unfortunately for my parents, they didn't have access to my monthly forecasts for myself. And after each failed meeting when we filed into the car, the boot was heavy with the weight of many disappointments.

In just a few short months into the process, it had rapidly come home to me that the toughest bit of the arranged marriage was not the gathering of courage for that very first meeting – hellish though it was – but finding a reserve of perseverance to attempt a second 'first' meeting, then a third 'first' meeting and so on without any end in sight. That was the actual gut-wrenching part. That was what brought most people to their knees, and I mean that quite literally. It made you want to pray, to want to desperately believe that there was a kind God with ADD out there and all you had to do was catch his eye, bring him to focus on your little problem and things would sort themselves out. They had to. For the sake of all three of us in that car, all dressed up on yet another Sunday morning, to go meet yet another seemingly eligible guy, for surely, this time it would be different, this time, we'd meet the one. It was debilitating, the frequent crashing of our collective expectations.

In the two and a half years that I spent meeting men my parents set me up with, I swung with Tarzan-like abandon between several coping mechanisms – if monopolizing friends' shoulders for bimonthly howls can indeed be called that. Some days I tried hard to imbibe Nichiren's Buddhist philosophy of being the change I wished to see in the world. I could have everything my heart desired, if only I believed I deserved it. To unlock my inner Buddha, my highest potential, I adopted Nichiren's mystic law, chanting the prescribed words, *Nam myoho renge kyo,* late into the night till I was hoarse. Then from time to time, in Sybilic fashion, my evil self would take over and I'd fling away all my newfound serenity, throwing a tantrum of elephantine proportions at my hapless parents who may have happened to suggest that I overlook a guy's height this once because everything else about him seemed so right. Sometimes, I'd just feel depressed and I'd escape to that happy place in my head, the writers' retreat in Italy, where no men, short or otherwise, were required. I wish I could've said that I approached my forty first-meetings with wisdom and grace, but on most days it was just long suffering sighs, and, hidden from plain view, a small, stubborn flicker of hope.

LET'S TALK ABOUT YOU AND ME

'Do you know why people clink glasses before taking their first sip?' I asked the curly-haired guy in front of me.

'I've never really thought about it,' he said.

'Well,' I began and pushed my coffee cup aside to remove all distraction, 'in the olden days, people often used poison to get rid of enemies. They'd invite them over for dinner and then instruct the servants to slip a little something into their food or wine and that's it – problem solved. No violence, no mess, no bloody hands. Eventually, people caught on and it became customary, as a show of good faith, for the host to clink glasses with his guests – the glasses would be filled to the brim, so that when they were clinked against each other the wine from the host's glass spilled into the guest's glass and vice versa. This way, the guests were assured that the wine was safe.'

'Oh, how interesting...'

'Yeah,' I continued enthusiastically, 'in fact, that's also the reason why you don't just put the glass down after clinking, you have to take a sip first, like everybody else.'

'Nice ... that's actually fun to know.'

'It is, right! Do you know why people shake hands when they mee...'

My phone buzzed and I paused mid-sentence to look at it. It was a message from my mother. 'WE CAN HEAR YOU', it said. I glanced sideways to look at the table about twenty feet away, where she was sitting with my father, making small talk with the guy's parents. I caught her eye and rolled my own exasperatedly, before turning back to my own conversation.

I have, what polite people would call, an outdoor voice. It is the pleasant and cultivated kind – at least that's what it sounds like in my head – but it is completely inappropriate for some situations. For example, when visiting someone in the ICU or discussing the wine menu with the maître d' of a fine-dining restaurant. I've always hated those girls who can sit right in front of you and conduct hour-long phone conversations with their boyfriends complete with giggles and fights, without you ever picking up a single, juicy word. When I need to have a private chat with somebody, I have to close the door and wait until everybody is watching *Comedy Circus* in another room. It's probably a genetic thing because everybody on my Dad's side of the family is loud. If you wanted to make a dark reality show, all you'd have to do is put a bunch of us together in a room and force us to play a game of Chinese whispers. We'd eventually kill each other.

While it had always been a bit of an inconvenience, my voice had never really bothered me until now. The decibel level at which I spoke was completely out of sync with the tenor of an arranged meeting.

Imagine this scenario: you're at a guy's house, sitting in the living room with his parents, your parents, the uncle and aunty who set you up, the guy's younger sister or cousin or both, who probably cut college because this promised to be far more educational, and the silent grandfather whose only job is to stare at everyone in the room intently and fathom their darkest secrets. You are looking down at your toes, waiting to speak until you've been spoken to – because you have learnt from previous experience that people don't expect you to break the ice – that particular job is for anybody else but you. The initial introductions are dispensed with and people have started to talk in smaller groups when the guy's mother takes the opportunity to lean forward and ask you softly, 'Beta, what exactly does a copywriter copy?'

'Copywriters don't copy anything, aunty. They write

ads – television commercials, radio jingles, hoardings, brochures – that sort of thing,' you say in the nicest possible way.

Only, it comes out much louder and can be heard over every other conversation in the room – everyone and I mean, everyone, even the maid who is serving tea and biscuits, stops what they are saying or doing and turns to look at you – your voice doesn't fit in with the demure, ladylike person who'd been sitting so quietly, with eyes downcast, for the last quarter of an hour. They stare at you curiously before eventually resuming their own conversations, but you can tell that they have made a mental note of it: *Loud voice. Hmmm ... what does that mean? Bold? Aggressive? Dominating?* They file it away for future inquiry.

You know when a person has been shot and is about to lose consciousness and you are asked to keep talking to them so that they don't black out and possibly die? That's how crucial conversation is to an arranged marriage meeting. Unlike any other kind of date which may lead up to marriage over the course of lingering dinners and late-night phone calls, both of you know that this could get there much, much quicker. You don't have the luxury to peel away layer after layer and slowly explore each other's personalities. At best, you have a few hours of unchaperoned conversation, during which you must try to ascertain: whether he has a sense of humour, what sort of father he'll make some day, whether he'll still have his hair in twenty years – basically everything you consider essential to your future wedded bliss.

Not only is it a bloody important conversation, but it also comes with a bit of a handicap – people don't always say what they mean. In their enthusiasm to create a good first impression, they may moderate their views or mask their true feelings. Both sides do it and neither may even be conscious of the deception, how then do you get the most out of that conversation? I suppose, you do it by paying attention to everything. From the volume they speak at and the accent they speak in to the questions they choose to ask and the answers they give to the ones you pose – everything they say or leave out reveals something about them.

So what do you talk about? You'd think that anything that came up naturally and helped you understand each other better would be a safe bet. But I have found that this can be a somewhat loose guideline. For instance, here's a conversation my best friend, Manan, had with a girl his folks had arranged for him to meet. He had just finished telling her that he wanted to make it clear from the start that he came from a family of modest means and that while he was doing well for himself now, he still lived in a rented apartment. In Mumbai, where life and limb were cheaper than real estate, and where the only thing more valuable than 100 sq ft. of land was 200 sq ft. of it, he'd often found his 'tenant status' to be a deal breaker.

Inspired by his forthrightness, the girl said, 'I want to share something with you too.'

Manan leaned forward expectantly, thinking that perhaps she wanted to talk about a previous relationship. It was only their first meeting and it was a little premature to be discussing past lovers, seeing as they had only just met and ordered their coffees, but she seemed determined to confess.

'Well, you should know that every time I am nervous...' she faltered.

He nodded encouragingly.

'Like, say, when I have exams or a job interview ... I ... I ... Every time I am nervous Igetloosemotions!' She said it in a big rush and then began to stare at her phone, turning red with every passing moment as if she was reading a lewd message on it.

It took Manan a few seconds to realize that she had just described a bowel condition.

'Oh,' he said, when it finally registered, and then for the lack of anything better to do, he took a sip of his tea.

A few seconds passed by quietly, then the girl excused herself to go to the ladies room and it took all of his self-restraint to not imagine why.

So what do you talk about? While doing some research for this book, I stumbled upon an illustrated article on wikiHow titled 'How to Talk in an Arranged Marriage

Meeting' in twenty-two steps. The existence of this piece really reassured me because it implied three things:

1. People actually googled such stuff, which meant that they had questions and doubts about arranged marriages and wanted answers.
2. The quality of the available advice left much to be desired.
3. There was obviously a great need for my tell-all book about arranged marriages in the market.

Here's what was at number 1: *Decide what kind of girl you want. Housewife, sweet and caring, family oriented, business women etc.* After all, how could a girl possibly be both, caring and a businesswoman? At number 15: *In life girls have fallen for a guy and a lot of girls repent for their mistake so don't instigate the past details.* So falling for a guy, any guy, is a blunder. Period. But hidden amongst these gems, at number 11 was: *Ask if the girl is open to change as your today needs may be a business women, 3 years from now the need will be for a caring mom and a caring daughter in law as your parents will be aging and 5 years from now the need will be of a house wife. See whether she is flexible.* However sexist and grammatically f***ed up, this is actually good advice – being upfront and clear about your expectations from your partner.

In fact, this was advice that would have stood me in good stead when I first started meeting men. As it was, I was somewhat in denial. Having agreed to go on dates set up by my parents, I wanted things to be as casual and date-like as they could possibly be. I wanted to talk about this and that, nothing that didn't come up naturally, nothing that would remind me that I hadn't just bumped into this young man at a bookstore and spontaneously been asked out for coffee. And certainly nothing that would remind me that I had met him on a matrimonial website.

RECOMMENDED CONVERSATION TOPIC #1 – EXPECTATIONS

Samit, a tall, light-eyed, plastic engineer, who got in touch with me on a popular matrimonial website, had studied and worked in Frankfurt for eight years before returning to India. Our first 'date' lasted two hours. He spoke of the work culture in Germany and how he had come to speak fluent German, while I spoke of my recent trip to Barcelona, my love affair with Gaudi's windows and how I had felt that Spanish was the most cheerfully robust language in the world. In our infatuation with all things European, we were as made for each other as Cinderella and her shoe. We agreed to meet a second time.

This time, it was another coffee followed by a long walk on Bandstand, a romantic promenade by the sea. We spoke of friends and the importance of having some. I spoke of my best friends and how I believed that the connections I shared with them were karmic in nature. He spoke of how he had found it difficult to reconnect with his old friends when he moved back to India and how he missed the friends he'd made in Germany. It rained that evening and as we walked under one umbrella, I couldn't help but think how perfect this was turning out to be.

We spent the next ten days texting and emailing each other occasionally, and then we met again.

'My parents would like to meet your folks,' I told him at the end of that date.

We'd enjoyed a leisurely lunch and had just finished discussing the weekend that had gone by – he'd gone on a two-day trek to Rajmachi, a popular trekking site a few hours away from Mumbai, and I'd watched *City of God* and *Children of Heaven* at an international film festival in the city. Now I had to reel our date back into the gambit of the arranged marriage.

'We don't have to decide immediately,' I told him. 'But my parents would be more comfortable once they've met you and your family, before things go any further.'

'So we can meet some more post that?'

'Yeah, absolutely ... I don't want to jump into anything either...'

'I'll speak to my parents. My Mum's been curious about you as well.'

'Super. Tell her Rana uncle will call.'

Through the great spidery Gujarati network, where someone always knows someone, my parents had found a common connection, a friend of one of my paternal uncles, who not only spoke well of Samit's family but agreed rather excitedly – as is usually the case with newly designated matchmakers – to set up a meeting between both families.

We met for tea and snacks at Rana uncle's house and spent that afternoon talking in separate groups – me with his Mum and mine, while he with the men. It was all very pleasant and that was the last I ever saw of Samit.

What happened? Yes, what the bloody hell happened was exactly what I wanted to know when I didn't hear from him for three days after the meeting. Our matchmaker, Rana uncle, was either very new at his job or didn't have very good news to share. In either case, things were silent at his end too. Finally, unable to bear the suspense, I asked my Dad to call him and get an update.

'They don't want to go ahead,' said our family friend, somewhat embarrassed, 'the family doesn't want a working daughter-in-law.'

There isn't a perfect word to describe that feeling between being surprised and being shocked, but maybe 'zapped' can convey how I felt. How had this not come up during our many coffee-fuelled conversations? We'd spoken about our jobs and described to each other the nuances of what we did for a living. But he'd never asked if I wanted to continue working post marriage and I, despite having friends who'd switched to being homemakers after marrying into conservative families, had just assumed that I'd continue along my chosen career path. And it wasn't until his Mum asked me what I planned to do after marriage had the topic been raised.

It would seem then that both Samit and I had set expectations and neither of us had thought to articulate them. I'd have saved myself some time and a lot of grief had I addressed things that were important, instead of trying to treat my arranged meeting like a first date.

Predictably, as with most things in life, there's another perspective to consider. My friend Trupti once met a guy, an animation artist, who conveyed to her within the first seven minutes of their meeting that he wanted a working wife.

'I am considering buying an apartment,' he informed her.

'Oh, that's nice. Where?' she asked.

'It's a small two BHK in Dombivli. But that means taking a home loan and that in turn means most of my income will be spent paying EMIs.'

Trupti nodded understandingly.

'So basically, I need my wife to provide for the day-to-day running of our home.'

He'd aired his expectations frankly, but it had given their meeting an almost transaction-like quality from the onset. If arranged marriage meetings were like multiple rounds of a job interview, this was like bringing up your salary expectations as soon as the interviewer had finished offering you coffee. It seems to me then that an honest discussion of expectations can be rewarding, but not before some sort of connection has been established. The two individuals have to develop at least an inkling of interest in each other before they begin to care about what the other person wants out of life and out of their partner.

Timing is not all, though. Expectations can be deal breakers, regardless of when they are aired because they simply may not be in sync.

A friend of a friend, Tejaswini, who works in advertising, was on her third date with a guy when he whipped out his childhood photos and showed them to her. He was as awkward, skinny and acne-ridden as most young boys are at fourteen.

'As you can see, I've come a long way from here,' he said.

She looked up grinning but was surprised to see that there was no trace of mirth on his face.

'Grooming is extremely important to me,' he continued, dead serious, 'mine, as well as my partner's...'

He paused and looked at her meaningfully.

'Okay...' said Tejaswini, wondering if she'd anything stuck in her teeth.

'Even in the middle of the night my wife should be spick and span,' he said.

'Spick and span?' asked Tejaswini, beginning to get a little annoyed.

'Yes,' he said and as he elaborated on how he expected his wife to have manicured nails, branded clothes and ironed hair at all times, she quickly realized that this wasn't about her or his future wife at all. He either placed just far too much importance on appearances or suffered from some kind of self-image complex. She saw that it might become an issue for them in the future and nipped the prospect in the bud.

When Kruti, a successful entrepreneur, met a VP of a private equity firm, things didn't even get as far as the second meeting. The VP was explicit. He didn't care whether the girl he married was educated or even literate, as long as she was open to staying at home and looking after his ailing mother.

'Basically, he wanted an unpaid nurse!' she announced furiously to her parents when she got back home.

'Isn't it a good thing then that he made it clear?' asked her mother wisely.

RECOMMENDED CONVERSATION TOPIC #2 – WORK

Work was usually safe ground. There was much you could tell about a guy from the way he spoke about his work. You got a measure of his passion and his ambitions, you could tell whether he was pragmatic or a burning idealist, whether he was a workaholic or if he believed in that elusive, almost mythical, work–life balance. Work was such a thoroughly illuminating topic that I always opened with it.

It was no different when I met Kavesh, an IITian, who'd recently quit his job to focus on his own start-up. I was looking forward to meeting him. It was such a novelty to meet an educated Gujarati boy who had made even the slightest unconventional career choice, that when he turned out to be good-looking as well, I slid into my chair most gleefully and ordered a cappuccino – '*Large, please.*'

'So Kavesh,' I said, stirring some sugar into my coffee, 'tell me a little bit about your start-up.'

Kavesh leant forward, cleared his throat and gazed so intensely into my eyes that I swear it made my heart flutter a little, and then, when he had my full attention he launched into a sales pitch.

He spoke of how he came up with the idea of making quirky T-shirts, who his partners were, how he went about sourcing the raw materials, where his manufacturing unit was located, who his designers were, what economies of scale he needed, how he planned to raise further capital, the hurdles he'd faced, how he planned to diversify the product range, where he stocked the final product, why e-retail was more efficient than in-store retail, how he wanted to use Facebook to promote the company and how he was in the process of finalizing a brand name. Finally, he asked, 'On that note, what do you think of the name "Jackfruit"?'

By this point, I was in a magnificent daze. As if spending Sunday afternoons meeting men my parents had picked wasn't bad enough, I had just sat through an hour-long proposal that had absolutely nothing to do with marriage. Kavesh was either not interested in tying the knot or not interested in tying the knot with me. As I left, I contemplated telling him that he should consider preparing a colourful PPT for his next meeting. He was good-looking but that wasn't enough of a visual aid. Not when you were making a girl feel about as invisible as a sounding board, and certainly not when you were using words like 'e-commerce' and 'financing model' on a weekend.

That evening, I called up my friend Sonal who was going through the wretched arranged marriage process herself and was sure to understand how dejected I felt.

'Did he mention Jackfruit?' she asked dryly, after I had finished giving her the gist of it.

As it turned out, she'd met Kavesh a few weeks ago and had been taken through his business plan in similar detail.

'It's like he is subconsciously using us for market research!' I said.

'We are his target audience, after all,' she said. 'Where else is he going to find such willing subjects and such qualitative answers?'

The next month, both Sonal and I received a friend request on Facebook from him, with an invitation to like his new page – Jackfruit. After that, we were not sure how subconscious it really was.

Mej, another friend, had the exact opposite experience when she met a guy who, when asked what he did for a living, said that he worked for the family business.

'So what aspect of the business are you involved in?' asked Mej. 'Are you responsible for marketing ... getting new clients...?'

'No, I have men to do that.'

'Purchase, then?'

'No, I have men to do that,' he said, and went silent again.

'Accounting? Do you get involved in the finance aspect of it?'

'No, I have men to do that.'

Mej went home that night and jokingly told her sister, 'Imagine if you married someone like that – on the wedding night, he may just say, "Wait, I have men to do that!"'

Of course, both of these are extreme examples, most men fall somewhere in between. But from the things they say and the things they leave out, their answers reveal something about who they are and what they hope to be. And it gives you a little to go on, something to base the life you're trying to imagine with a complete stranger.

RECOMMENDED CONVERSATION TOPIC #3 – INTERESTS

It was important to talk about interests for many reasons, the most critical of which was to see if the opposite side had any. Mej once met a guy, an intense-looking PhD scholar, who when asked what his interests were went quiet for a full five minutes before replying, 'I used to play cricket in school.'

I'd gone through enough biodatas to know that an astonishingly large percentage of the Indian male population considered 'going on long drives' to be a valid interest. Now, I'm hardly in any position to be judgemental about how people pass their time, seeing that a huge chunk of my adult life has been spent in and outside trial rooms at malls, but I don't list 'running up a credit card bill' as an interest. An interest should add another dimension to your personality, and it was important for me that the person I was with had rich and varied interests. They didn't have to be the same as mine, but I hoped their interests would be 'interesting', like gardening or astronomy. I knew zilch about either, but there was beauty involved in the pursuit of them. Through my life partner I hoped to glimpse new worlds, maybe learn to identify the bear or wolf or some other sparkling carnivore in the sky, or just get my hands dirty tending a pot of cherry tomatoes. I also wanted to share my own worlds with him – introduce him to a new author or to the joys of exploring a new city on foot. Which is why, every time I met a new guy, I always asked, 'So, what do you do with your free time?' Seemingly simple, in reality it was a loaded question. I was not only trying to see how 'interesting' he was and how open to trying new things, but also trying to find out if he was constitutionally passionate. I wanted to see if his eyes shone or if he smiled involuntarily with pleasure or spoke just a wee bit louder in his excitement when he told me about his favourite interest. After all, I figured, if he couldn't feel strongly about the things he supposedly enjoyed doing, how would he feel passionate about me?

However, I have learnt since that people are not a neat sum of their parts. Here's a conversation a friend of mine had with a girl his parents had arranged for him to meet. The girl was part of the rather well-regarded leadership programme at GE in the United States and when they spoke about their respective jobs, he was happy to see that she spoke about hers with gusto and enthusiasm. At some point, he asked her, 'So what do you do when you aren't working?'

'Oh, I enjoy reading and watching TV,' she said.

An avid reader himself, my friend was delighted. 'What sort of books?'

'Well, I just finished reading the new book on Warren Buffet and now I am reading Jack Welch's *Winning*.'

'Business books ... That's great, what else?'

'Not much else...' she said, appearing genuinely puzzled.

'What about TV, what shows do you like?'

'CNBC. I can watch it 24/7! And I absolutely love Jim Cramer,' she said, referring to his popular show on investment advice – *Mad Money*.

It seems then that a great passion for one area in one's life doesn't always translate into a passion for life itself.

In fact, it can limit the enjoyment of life by narrowing our experiences of it. Pretty deep, huh? Thank you, there's more.

While it was great to meet people who were passionate about their interests, it was equally important that the said interests be compatible with yours. A fact that was rapidly brought home to me when I met a stockbroker who said he traded in futures and options, a volatile and high-risk stock market division.

'So what do you do with your free time?' I asked him, eventually.

'I catch up with my friends.'

'And what do you guys do?'

'We play Flush,' he said, referring to the card game popularly known as teen patti.

'What else?'

'Well, sometimes we also play poker – one of my friends has just bought a professional Texas Hold 'em set from the US.'

'That sounds like fun. So do you guys play with money?'

'Of course, what fun is the game otherwise?'

I laughed and agreed with him. I enjoyed the occasional poker night myself, and could vouch that people only played seriously when there was some money involved.

'How about travelling?' I asked him to steer the conversation in another direction.

'Oh, I enjoy holidays.'

A travel buff myself, I said, 'That's great. So where did you go last?'

'Goa. They have such a great casino there! We gambled all night.'

'That sounds like fun,' I said, beginning to have a sinking suspicion that there wasn't a whole lot more to this guy other than a passion for high stakes and the ensuing adrenaline rush.

He continued, 'Yeah, in fact, now my friends and I are planning a trip to Hong Kong, just to visit the casinos in Macau. We hear they are as good as the ones in Vegas!'

'Sounds exciting,' I said, not excited in the least.

HERE'S A LONGER LIST OF THINGS YOU PROBABLY SHOULDN'T SAY

'Do you think it's okay to have an extramarital relationship?'

A girl asked my cousin this question at their first arranged meeting. Yep. True story. Now, I've lambasted him a hundred times for not having gotten to the bottom of that question. He was simply too taken by surprise to ask any follow-ups. But I can't help but wonder what the girl had been on about. It seemed terrible timing to try to gauge someone's views on open marriage and infidelity with their parents sitting just twenty feet away, at the next table. Not to mention that this was in the first fifteen minutes of the meeting in the first place.

'Assuming you were the mayor of Mumbai city, what would you change about it?'

I just have one question for the guy who asked my cousin Charu this: '*Who have you assumed you are? A judge at the Miss World beauty pageant?'*

'So, are you a Jain-Jain?'

'So no onions, huh?' asked the curly-haired engineer in front of me with raised eyebrows.

'Nope,' I said.

'And garlic? What about garlic?'

'Nope.'

'Like never ever?' he asked, apparently intrigued.

'Not never ... just not if I can help it,' I said, trying to be as brief as possible.

'So you are like a Jain-Jain?'

'Uh-uh,' I agreed.

'Don't you ever get tempted?' he asked, completely undeterred by my short answers.

'I don't like the taste ... so, no.'

'Tell me you are kidding ... who doesn't like garlic? I mean garlic bread ... come on!' He almost salivated into his coffee cup.

I gave him a small smile and attempted to change the subject back to his experiences in his hostel, which we'd been discussing earlier. 'It must have been difficult to come by good food in the hostel, right?'

'Yeah, it was pretty bad,' he said, 'but hang on, how do you manage without garlic when you are travelling?'

I sighed. This was such an inanely pointless line of conversation that it amazed me at the regularity with which it crept up in the course of my arranged meetings. Surely, in the limited time you had to judge whether the opposite person was potential life-partner material, there were more important discussions to be had than how they seasoned their food?

'I am not looking to get married.'

Once, halfway into a meeting, the guy casually mentioned to me that he wasn't really interested in getting married just then, and that he'd only agreed to the meeting because his parents had insisted. Then, he'd proceeded to tell me about how he spent his Saturdays, as if he actually thought I would still be interested to know.

'Aren't you tempted to have one-night stands?'

Jharna, a friend of mine, who manages a logistics company, travels a lot for work. She was once describing her job to a guy she'd just met, when he wanted to know that since she travelled abroad frequently, if she'd ever been tempted to have one-night stands. The question was not only intrusive, but also absurd. He had simply assumed that the number of visa stamps on one's passport must have a direct correlation with one's propensity for promiscuity.

'I am on a diet.'

A young, 200-pound businessman made this announcement on a coffee date with Charu. While there is absolutely nothing wrong with this particular statement, it's just not entirely convincing if you follow it by sucking up the last few drops of your chocolate fudge cold coffee with the straw.

'So ... why are you still single?'

Kruti, who is thirty-four, has been meeting men for more than half a decade but is still to find Mr Right. It riles her when the men she meets – who are in their mid- to late thirties themselves – think it falls in the realm of suitable small talk to ask her why she is still single. How is she meant to respond? Is this her cue to break down and divulge all the gory details of a previous failed relationship? Or admit to secretly being afflicted by male pattern baldness? Or is this meant as a backhanded compliment? Does it imply: 'I'm surprised you're still single despite being so attractive'? How have they imagined this conversation to go?

Guy: So Kruti, why are you still single?

Kruti: I don't know ... I think I've just been waiting for you to show up all my life.

Is that what they're after then? Or have they simply not thought it through? Because when Kruti throws the question back at them, which is how she usually responds, the same guys just shrug and say, 'Dunno, didn't meet the right person I guess.' Well, duh.

MANNERS MAKETH A MATCH

Arranged marriage meetings are complex social situations that often involve more than two people and are subject to multiple egos, expectations and temperaments. For the meetings to go smoothly, it may help to have a list of good practices, a sort of code of conduct. Of course, for it to make any difference at all, both parties should have read this book.

One Sunday afternoon, my parents and I hauled ourselves into the family car and drove all the way across the city for fifty minutes to get to the cafe of the Holiday Inn at Juhu beach. We were supposed to be meeting the parents of a guy who worked in Houston and who was scheduled to come to Mumbai a month later. They'd picked the place. We reached at the agreed upon time and after we'd washed the grime of the city off our faces, we settled in to wait. They arrived a full twenty minutes late.

'So sorry to keep you waiting!' boomed the guy's father as he sucked in his huge belly to squeeze into the seat opposite my Dad.

'No problem,' said my father, 'we all know how lazy Sunday afternoons can be.'

I glared at him – what was that supposed to mean? *We are perfectly happy to wait while you finish your Sunday siesta?* I hated it when he was so accommodating just because the person who'd kept him waiting was related to the 'prospective candidate'. Under any other circumstance, my Dad was the most impatient man I knew.

'Isn't it funny that those who live the closest are always the last to arrive?' said the guy's father, chuckling.

'You live nearby then?' asked my mother.

'Nearby?' he said, grinning at his wife and daughter as if he'd just heard the funniest thing in the world. 'We live in the building right across the street!'

'Good, good,' said my father smiling pleasantly and passed him the menu. 'Shall we order something?' *Seriously, sometimes I didn't recognize the man.*

We placed our orders and chatted for a bit. The conversation largely involved the guy's father holding forth on how great the United States was and how dismal things were in India. Every time he stopped, I thought he would burst into the 'Star Spangled Banner', but he just took a big gulp of his cold coffee, while the mother took the opportunity to ask me inconsequential details about myself.

'How do you commute to work, beta?'

'I take the train.'

'Do you believe in Lord Ganesha?'

'Who doesn't, aunty?'

'True, true … I am a big bhakt.'

Since there was to be no 'date part' of the meeting, in about thirty minutes we had run out of things to say to each other and soon it was time to leave. My father called for the bill. The waiter placed it perfectly at the centre of the two men. My father reached for the bill while the boy's father looked away and took another noisy sip of his rather tall glass of coffee. After the waiter had brought back the change, we said our goodbyes. They promised to get in touch when their son was in the city. And then my parents and I filed into the car and spent an hour and a half getting back home.

Their behaviour was in such spectacular bad form that it was as if the Universe knew that I'd write this book some day and would need a sufficiently abominable example to illustrate my point. To understand the many different ways this family screwed up, let's break up a meeting into its basic elements:

1. The choice of venue

You'd think it was a matter of common courtesy that in a busy city like Mumbai – beleaguered as it was with its chronic bad traffic and awful pockmarked roads – the place chosen to meet was equidistant or at least equally convenient for both parties concerned. And yet the Houston family – I'll call them that for ease of reference – picked a cafe that was a hop away for them and a hike away for us. Their behaviour was so presumptuous that it bordered on insulting. Was our time not as valuable as theirs? Or did they think, in their secure position as the parents of the boy, that our need was greater than theirs? I was furious with my parents for having agreed to go all the way to their doorstep. Ours was a progressive community. Gujarati girls were increasingly well educated and given all the opportunities and resources that were available to the boys. But when it came to marriage, the general mindset seemed to be that the parents of the girl had more at stake than those of the boy. My parents would probably deny the suggestion, but think about the kind of treatment they had tolerated – not only had the opposite side come twenty minutes late, but they had done so without taking the trouble to think up a valid excuse. No 'Sorry, Akshay Kumar had come to the building and we couldn't get past the fans' or 'Sorry, our dog swallowed the house keys and we were waiting for him to shit them out.' They offered no good reason, just a casual, offhand apology, knowing fully well that there would be no repercussions whatsoever – they were, after all, the boy's parents.

2. Punctuality

As in any social situation, turning up at a mutually agreed upon time conveys respect for your own word as well as consideration for the other person's time. Punctuality is the basic tenet of good form and yet the arranged marriage landscape is fraught with stories of people kept waiting for no apparent good reason other than casual tardiness.

Jharna and her parents were once invited to meet a guy and his family at their home. They waited for the guy in the family living room for over an hour, while his parents made desperate small talk because the guy had 'forgotten' about the meeting and had gone off to the gym instead.

Tejaswini recounts an instance when she was supposed to meet a guy from Canada who was visiting Mumbai for a short while and had put up at the ITC Sheraton in Parel. It was 9:30 a.m. on a Sunday morning and he'd invited her to breakfast. She reached the hotel at the designated hour but there was no sign of the guy nor any message. She waited in the lobby for fifteen minutes, after which she called him.

'Gosh, I overslept!' he said groggily when he picked up the phone, and then kept her waiting for another half an hour while he showered and got ready for their meeting.

But that wasn't all. Once he'd apologized and they'd settled at their table in the coffee shop, he offered her coffee. 'I am not a breakfast person at all,' he said, after he'd given the menus back to the waiter, 'but if you'd like something to go with it, we can always order.'

Tejaswini who was very much a breakfast person and who hadn't eaten anything in the delusion that this was a breakfast date, eventually had half a coffee which she insisted on paying for before making a fuming exit.

3. Getting the bill

When my parents and I met a guy and his family, I was always interested in seeing whether the guy's father reached for the bill. Indian society has always been gaga about the male heir, and even now, it is always the girl who is considered 'lucky' to have made a good match. In this context, when the boy's family offered to get the bill, it indicated more than just good manners – it, hopefully, implied a progressive bent of mind.

Note, I say 'offer' because that was about as far as my father would let them go before he'd snatch the bill folder, slip in the cash and hand it back to the waiter. For all my insistence on a forward-looking family, my own parents believed that it was more appropriate for the girl's side to pay, and all my attempts at questioning this were met with a highly unsatisfactory 'That's how things are supposed to be' followed by an infuriatingly dismissive 'You won't understand'.

It was true, I didn't understand. I didn't understand how anyone could behave like the Houston father and sit back indifferently, while someone they'd only just met paid for their and their family's – even those who brought along extended families expected to be treated – cold coffees. I didn't understand what gave them the obnoxious sense of entitlement that they didn't feel the need to even pretend to reach for their wallets. I didn't understand why I should even have to consider getting married into a family where people lacked such a basic form of courtesy. Much to my parents' dismay, I made 'did they at least offer' one of the criteria by which I decided if I wanted to meet someone a second time.

Now, if I've given the impression that all of the families we encountered were moochers, that really wasn't the case. There were some who would offer graciously and my father would decline with equal grace, and it would all be very agreeable. But the experiences were so few and far between that when we met a family who had actually arrived at the cafe before us and given the waiter their credit card to take care of the bill in advance, I was mighty impressed and the first thing I did when I got home was write about it in my diary.

Now, you may not realize it, but it is a big deal to get into my diary, mainly because I am an exceptionally lazy journal keeper and only a few of the forty-odd men I met ever made it in there. What's more, I can't find that diary now, and the fact that I still remember the credit card family, almost six years since we met them, says something, doesn't it?

I must mention at this point that the at-least-offer-to-get-the-bill directive is applicable to all parties concerned. Guys doing the rounds of the arranged marriage circuit often complain that for all their 'independence and feminism', the girls they are set up with rarely offer to split the bill.

Ladies, I realize that we're used to having our dates pay for our drinks, but let's face it, this is not really a date, is it? The guy didn't see you at a bar and send the waiter over with another one of whatever it was you were having. He doesn't intend to come at you with a swagger and a corny pickup line in the hope of scoring your phone number. That, he already has. In all probability, he is only here because your kundlis – the astrological charts that mapped the position of the planets at the time of one's birth – matched, your biodata seemed suitable and his parents asked him to go. He is not motivated by the prospect of getting into your pants, not in the near future at least. This is most likely as tedious for him as it is for you. Really, it is only fair that you at least 'offer' to share the tab.

OTHER THINGS TO KEEP IN MIND

The appropriateness of the venue is as important as its convenience.

One Saturday afternoon, I was supposed to be meeting a diamond trader. Since it was a working day for him, I had offered to let him decide a convenient time and place.

'Let's meet below my office building,' he said, 'and we can head somewhere from there.'

The 'somewhere' turned out to be an udipi opposite his office. For those of you unfamiliar with the concept of an udipi restaurant, let me paint you a little picture: an udipi is a fast food joint that serves mainly south Indian cuisine. It has narrow tables packed in cramped rows, which smell stale like the mops that are used to clean them. The waiters wear dirty grey – I mean the colour, they may or may not actually be dirty – uniforms and descend upon you with laminated menu cards before your bottom has even touched the seat. The food is served to you in steel plates which you are better off not scrutinizing too closely. At peak hours, there is always a throng of people waiting outside the restaurant for their turn to get in. If you are a single diner, it is perfectly possible that you will be asked to scoot over and share your table. The pace of service is brisk and its tone no-nonsense. The busboy tries to clear your plate while you are still fingering the last morsel of your dosa. And the waiter leaves you a little chit with your tab on it even before you've made up your mind on whether you want to have dessert. Am I putting you off an udipi? Because that was not the point – the food is not only affordable but absolutely delicious. But to pick it as a spot for an arranged meeting where you needed to talk to the other person at length and in peace – and air conditioning is not a substitute for ambience – was about as appropriate as trying to conduct a sarangi recital at a fish market.

Girls much prefer it if you look at their face during a conversation.

My friend – who prefers not to be named – was once set up with a corporate banking guy who couldn't keep his eyes off her chest.

'We'd be talking about his work or my photography and his eyes would just slide down and quickly back up again. Down and up. Down and up. It was so embarrassing!' she called to tell me when she got back from that meeting.

'That sounds horrible. You should've gotten up and left!'

'I would've! But Samita aunty, who set us up, is such a good friend of my mother's.'

'So then?'

'Then, nothing ... I had to place the menu card strategically between us!'

Besides making things uncomfortable for my friend, this kind of behaviour was also difficult to explain to Samita aunty, who couldn't understand why in the world she didn't want meet that nice young man again.

Again: Girls much prefer it if you look at their face during a conversation.

Jharna once sat through a coffee where the guy spent more time checking out a group of girls sitting at the next table than talking to her. Needless to say, it was a very, very quick coffee.

You don't comment on a girl's weight. Ever.

Once, on a third date with a guy, a friend of mine decided to buy herself an ice cream. They were walking along Marine Drive, things were going well and it seemed like the perfect weather to have a scoop of Tender Coconut. She was halfway through the ice cream when the guy asked for her cone.

Thinking that maybe he wanted a bite, she handed it over, but to her surprise he said, 'I think you're done,' and dumped her ice cream in the bin.

She stared at him, too amazed to say anything.

'Small portion sizes,' he said by way of explanation, 'is the key to losing weight.'

That, actually, is also the key to losing a girl.

This doesn't really belong here or anywhere else for that matter, but it is too absurd to not mention.

My cousin and his parents were once invited to meet a girl at her home. The girl was late getting home from work, so they passed the time by making small talk in the living room and munching on savouries. When the doorbell finally rang, a girl entered and the girl's father jumped up exclaiming, 'That's Sangeeta's twin sister' – then turning to my cousin – 'why don't you chat with her instead, Sangeeta looks exactly the same!' True story.

IT'S ELEMENTARY, MY DEAR WATSON

An arranged marriage is risky business. There is way too much at stake on a decision that is based neither on past experience, nor on learning, nor on foreknowledge. When you opt for an arranged marriage, there's no dry run or probation period. No let's-hook-up-a-few-times-and-take-it-from-there or let's-live-in-together-and-see-how-we-feel. It's like signing up for tandem skydiving with only one parachute. There's no backup of previous promises, dates and anniversaries or of shared memories, laughs and dreams. In fact, there's nothing to fall back on except sheer luck and some amount of due diligence. A little bit of poking around and a lot of good old praying.

Traditionally, due diligence for an arranged alliance

involved tapping into the fine mesh of extended family, friends, business associates and neighbours that formed the fabric of Indian society. At one time, not much escaped the wide orbit of people around a family. If there was a tale to tell, it was duly noted, repeated and passed on. Every family had a set of unofficial, self-designated chroniclers, people who'd known them for generations and could, if called upon, recount the highs and lows with just the right amount of relish. In those days, memories were long and the collective consciousness of society was enduring and, to a large extent, even reliable. Marriages were arranged within neat, Russian doll-like sets of castes, sects and subsects. If there was anything worth knowing about a potential candidate, it would be brought to your attention – by a minimum of three sources at least.

While this may still be true of most Indian small towns and cities, in the bigger metros the gap between people's public and private lives is ever widening. People are busier, more involved and interested in their online social networks than in the world around them. Priorities have been changing – while religion remains an important criterion, sects and subsects of castes are fast losing their relevance in a world where educational qualifications, professional designations and even accents have become powerful class indicators and dividers. What's more, proposals are no longer bound by geography. Alliances are sought and entertained from across different cities, countries and even continents. Matchmaking is no longer the sole domain of your friendly neighbourhood aunty brigade. There are professional bureaus, matrimonial websites as well as regional and national newspapers bursting with classifieds under 'Brides wanted' and 'Grooms wanted'. All of which in effect means that the available information about a potential candidate is no longer exclusively first-hand. Sure, you'll still find someone who knows someone who knows the opposite side. But how can you be certain that the family in question isn't a bunch of raving, Asaram Bapu-worshipping lunatics? Well, you can't, at least not a cent per cent.

Historically, the onus for due diligence rests squarely on the shoulders of parents. Having taken on the responsibility of finding their offspring a spouse, they must now ensure that the prospective bride or groom is suitable looking, appropriately educated, settled in his or her career and that the family in question has a background, reputation and lifestyle to match their own. It is a critical role and most parents approach it with a curious mixture of zeal and trepidation. On the one hand, they want to unearth everything of consequence about a said family, but on the other, they sincerely hope that their search has come to an end, that this candidate who seems so suitable in every respect might really be the one. It is a hard job, for they must try to find skeletons in a closet, which they are hoping to god won't have any.

Parents go about the task by making calls, tapping contacts and conducting a series of direct or indirect inquiries. Sometimes, this approach works effectively. Calls can reveal temperamental mothers-in-law, financial difficulties, undisclosed reasons for previously broken engagements or, as in the case of my friend Karishma, a guy who considered denims unsuitable for girls from 'cultured' families.

But sometimes, parents go overboard and their inquiries can hinder their cause rather than help. Here's a conversation that the mother of a girl had with my cousin in response to a classified ad they'd posted for his younger brother.

Mother: So, do you have an apartment in Mumbai?

Brother: In Navi Mumbai, yes.

Mother: Is that where you currently stay?

Brother: D, as you know, stays in New York. We stay in Goregaon – it's closer to work.

Mother: Is that apartment rented?

Brother: Yes.

Mother: How many bedrooms?

Brother: Two and a half.

Mother: How many people?

Brother: Two.

Mother: How many square feet is it?

At which point, my cousin very politely told her to send across her daughter's biodata, and should it seem suitable – almost certain that it wouldn't – they could have the first meeting in the said apartment itself.

Mej recalls a conversation she had with the mother of a boy who called to speak to Mej's Mum, but found herself talking to Mej instead. The sole purpose of her three-minute call seemed to be to find out if Mej was slim.

'Will you describe yourself to me, beta?'

'Uh ... I could send you a picture, aunty.'

'No, no. Just tell me, are you tall, short, slim ... are you slim?'

'Yeah, I guess. I have an average build.'

'Good, good. My son is very slim, so it is important I find a thin girl for him. Do you exercise?'

'I go for walks a few days a week.'

'Yes, walking is very good, keeps the figure in check ... so what did you say your height was?'

'5 ft 6 in. aunty, can I ask Mummy to send you my biodata?'

'Yes, yes, please do that ... 5 ft 6 in. is a good height for a girl. These days all the girls seem to be so tall and slim.'

She continued asking Mej a bunch of questions, half of which involved trying to gauge her weight, and was only satisfied when an exasperated Mej assured her that she was as slim as Bipasha Basu and, like Mej told her mother later, about as likely to entertain a proposal from the lady's son.

In both the above instances, the answers were important to the parents, but maybe there are other ways of arriving at them.

Here's an out-of-the-box approach. The father of a girl once asked Prashant, a friend who works in advertising, for the reference of his previous employer. Prashant was used to spending long hours at work and the father figured that if there was anybody who could have no vested interest in talking-up Prashant it was someone he no longer worked for. The father called Prashant's ex-boss and asked for an appointment. It was unusual, but Prashant and his boss had parted on good terms and the boss agreed to the meeting. The girl's parents showed up on the designated day and spent an hour with the boss discussing Prashant's work habits, his temperament and the nature of the advertising industry in general. Advertising is a glamorous industry, fraught with a reputation of fostering alcohol binges, drug abuse and promiscuity. The parents wanted to know how much of it was true and how much of it applied to Prashant. The boss put their mind at ease and the meeting ended with a tour of the office.

And here's another. When the parents of a girl accompanied her to my friend Tinu's house for a third meeting, the mother, albeit very hesitantly, inquired if they could possibly see the certificates of all the degrees that Tinu had mentioned in his biodata. It was an unconventional request, but the arranged marriage landscape is rife with stories where computer software diplomas are passed off as engineering degrees and receptionists refer to themselves as 'Executive at an MNC'. And while there's nothing wrong with either holding a diploma or being a receptionist, the information provided paints such a different impression that it is best to do a bit of digging of your own.

As with everything else in life, when it comes to digging, there's a fine line you are better off not crossing. For instance, the parents of the girl my friend's friend, Maanav, was engaged to, asked him to send them copies of his salary slips. It was not only too direct a request but also ill timed, they were going to be married in a month. It annoyed Maanav so much that he almost called off the engagement.

In the twenty-first century, additional help comes from unexpected quarters. Online social networks are complete worlds within themselves and virtual lives can sometimes be a more accurate portrayal of an individual's thoughts and actions than reality itself. Young people about to be set up on arranged dates have taken to scouring the web for additional information about the person they are about to meet.

When I first started meeting men, Orkut was still breathing its last in India. Everybody had gotten themselves Facebook profiles, but you still logged on to your Orkut page, out of sheer habit. I was supposed to meet Sagar, a chartered accountant, through a popular matrimonial website. He had put up a decent bio of himself along with a pleasant picture. We exchanged a few messages through the website, before deciding to switch to emails and Gchat. His email ID with the words 'head', 'bang' and 'death' strung together without spaces should've been my first hint that things may not be as they seemed. But I chalked it up to a heavy metal thing, exchanged phone numbers with him and decided on a time and place to meet. And then, as an afterthought I logged onto his Orkut profile. The page was filled with pictures of skulls and bones, abusive posts in filthy language and the word 'Satan' that popped up frequently and randomly without context. Suffice it to say that Sagar didn't seem like the kind of nice young man I wanted to take home to meet my parents. I made up an excuse and cancelled our meeting, only to have him call me that night, slurring, incoherent and piss drunk.

Tejaswini recalls the time she was supposed to meet a guy who worked in the construction business. The pictures attached with his biodata suggested chiselled good looks and she was rather looking forward to their meeting. On the eve of their coffee date, she went online to see if she could learn more about him. His LinkedIn profile turned out to be a delight. Clean-shaven and in a suit, he looked every bit the savvy businessman his impressive resume suggested he was. Excited, Tejaswini logged onto Facebook and went to his profile. In those days, Facebook's privacy settings were not as unhelpful as they are now. Which meant you didn't have to be friends with someone just to get access to their personal lives. Tejaswini believes she owes Mark Zuckerberg one for that. The 'construction guy' had put up a profile picture of himself in a slinky, yellow vest with holes in it – think Amir Khan in *Rangeela* – only the effect was far from comic. With his arm at his waist, biceps bulging and him looking intensely at the camera, it seemed more like a portfolio picture of a B-grade model. Distressed, Tejaswini quickly went to his other albums to see if there was any redeeming explanation, only to discover more pictures of him in body-hugging, V-necked T-shirts and shirts with buttons left open to reveal a hairless chest, posing with – and this was the most alarming bit of it all – other men in similarly fashioned attire. It was with a sinking feeling in her stomach that she realized that he was most likely gay.

APPARENTLY, THE STARS SAID SO

When I turned twenty, an age my father considered appropriate for marriage, he made a beeline for the family astrologer. I was just about to finish college and in my father's eyes if you were old enough to get a BA, you must be old enough to get a husband. So he dug up my janam kundli, and put down a list of questions to ask the astrologer. 'Would I have a "love marriage" or an "arranged marriage?"' was the first thing he wanted to know. A previous, failed three-year-long relationship may have put it in his head that if I could sneak behind his back and have one affair, I could do it again. The astrologer assured him that it would be arranged, that my 'lagn yog', that period when the stars were aligned favourably for marriage, would start the year after and that I would find a good husband soon. My father came home with a spring in his step and encouraged my mother to make an exploratory round of the jewellery stores. Unfortunately for him though, he chose not to tell me about the prediction. Thus oblivious to how my future was *supposed* to pan out, I made my own plans and got a master's degree and a career instead. It was all very worrying for him because by the time I finally agreed to go on an arranged meeting, I had skipped an entire lagn yog, as well as the lean year that followed, and was about to enter the second, and most likely final, lagn yog of my life. I was twenty-four. Needless to say, the person most excited to be ordering a cappuccino on my very first arranged coffee date was my father.

Then, as it so often happens to people who are twenty-four, a year went by and I turned twenty-five. There had been several coffee dates but none that made you want to go home and tell your parents, 'Could you please call his parents.' My father got very nervous.

'But it was supposed to happen quickly!' he finally confided in me. 'It will be very sudden, the astrologer had said.'

He fretted and then naturally, I fretted. Because if the astrologer had said it, it really should've happened. I put a great deal of faith in the forces that ruled the cosmos. The Universe, I believed, knew things that I didn't. The planets and stars held bimonthly strategy meets to chalk out the path to my future. So what was up? Why weren't things going according to plan?

My faith in the arts and sciences of divination was in direct proportion to my fascination with it, which was immense. An astrologer I had once gone to meet put it down to the heavy influence of Saturn on my chart. Apparently, people who had a strong Shani were not only inexplicably attracted to the occult sciences, but also good at practising them. Armed with that knowledge, I had studied tarot for an entire year. I would rush after work for my private tutorial, make copious notes of everything my teacher said and practise relentlessly on unwitting family, friends and anyone at all who betrayed a mere flicker of curiosity while I shuffled my big deck of purple cards. Then, one of my readings turned out to be eerily true. It was a general spread for a colleague's love life but the cards indicated a conflict in her relationship and pointed towards another woman as the cause.

'That doesn't sound like us,' she said, when I told her what I saw in the cards.

'Good! I am glad!' I said, relieved. 'Like I told you, I am still learning.'

That night though, she called and confessed, in between sobs, that things had indeed been rocky. There had been graphic dreams of an ex-girlfriend amongst other ongoing melodrama.

'You were bang on,' she said, before hanging up.

She meant it as a compliment but I couldn't enjoy it. It was not a good feeling. In fact, it terrified me. I didn't really want to know somebody's future, let alone mine. Tarot had been fun while it lasted, but it seemed the time had come to get myself a new hobby.

I only mention this little episode to paint a picture of just how seriously I took these things. A face reader once visited our office and I loitered outside the conference room for a whole hour because I couldn't muster the courage to hear what he had to say.

So seeing how things stood with astrology and me, it is hardly surprising that I took this prediction about my marriage very seriously.

'Let's get a second opinion,' I announced to my parents.

'Yes, let's,' my father agreed, immediately.

'If we must,' my mother said resignedly. She had this whole it-will-happen-when-it's-meant-to theory going and believed that all I needed to do was keep looking. Apparently, the time I spent in deep philosophical consultation with astrologers would be better spent sipping lattes with prospective grooms. She was naive that way, my mother. So off we went from one astrologer to another.

'Look outside your community,' said one.

'She will settle abroad,' said another.

And to each of them I asked, 'Love or arranged?' Perennially hopeful that unbeknownst to me, love was lurking just round the corner, biding its time until it was sure I would really appreciate it when I bumped into it. I wanted my brush with arranged marriage to be just that, experiences that would ultimately give my grand love story the depth and drama it deserved. But the answer never changed.

'He'll be tall,' said a foot reader, 'working in finance or something related.'

Now, I realize that a 5 ft 7 in. girl looking to get married to a Gujarati boy, wasn't very likely to end up with a short wedding-band guitarist in any case. Gujarati men are never encouraged to think of music as a serious career option.

> Kalpesh: Papa (*pronounced puppa*), I'd like to become a percussionist.
>
> Papa: That's great, Kalpu. I am going to send you to Trinity College in London to study music.

This kind of conversation is simply unheard of in a Gujarati household. Even those who do get away with it, have probably heard:

Tabla? Learn your tables first, we'll see about the tabla.

The foot reader – who studied my big toe with such interest that I promised myself I would never be lazy about getting a pedicure again – was probably just making an educated guess. But at that point I so badly wanted to believe in something or somebody that you could've told me I'd marry an astronaut and I'd have promptly fantasized about a sangeet sandhya on the moon.

For those of you who've never attended a Gujarati sangeet sandhya – and really, what kind of social pariah has never been invited to a Gujju wedding? You seriously need to up the game and get yourself some Gujarati friends pronto – this is a pre-wedding music function that involves the chief members of the wedding party taking turns to perform to hit Bollywood dance numbers. It is all very exciting. In fact, I'd say, it's the most amount of fun one can have at a social gathering without alcohol – okay, barring maybe a Rahul Gandhi rally. To begin with, everyone comes prepared. They've practised their moves – yes, even the ones who look like they are having coordinated paralytic seizures – with a professional choreographer for months in advance. Then there's a DJ who arrives equipped with a foam machine, pink disco lights and a repertoire of the choicest item numbers about disreputable ladies called Munni, Sheila and Chameli, because somehow that seems like appropriate music to play in a gathering that includes little children and even littler grannies. Then there are the ear-hair-sprouting uncles and the jiggly-armed aunties who in the normal order of things wouldn't dream of holding hands with their spouses in public, but when called upon to perform at a sangeet sandhya think nothing of getting cosy with each other on stage in touchy-feely 'cupple songs'. Then there're always someone's chubby, pimply, pre-pubescent kids who dance for the entire six-minute duration of a song and their father will inevitably yell encore at the end and then they dance the six whole minutes again. And finally, the bride and the groom are summoned for their own duet performance, which for some reason the MC – an enthusiastic member of the family with a latent Dale Carnegie syndrome from whom the mike will eventually have to be yanked away with some force at the end of the evening – always describes as a solo, as if the couple is one beating heart with four flailing limbs. Once the couple is on stage, all eyes are usually on the bride who has been starving herself for months, having followed up the chew-the-watermelon-seeds-diet with suck-the-core-of-the-apple-diet, and is as a result looking so gorgeous that everyone in the audience, even the women, can't find anything snotty to say about her dancing.

Like I said, sangeet sandhyas are brilliant and really the main reason I wanted to be married in the first place. Okay, maybe not the main but you have to admit that a thousand pair of eyes following every swish and twirl of your ghaghra while you danced to 'Mehendi laga ke rakhna' was the stuff Indian girls' dreams were made of. On second thoughts, maybe I should've spent my energies getting Yash Chopra to cast me in one of his films, because finding a husband was definitely proving to be tougher than breaking into Bollywood.

'It is because of her "kaal sarp dosh",' announced one pandit ominously, when my parents asked him why it was taking me so long to meet someone suitable. 'Surely, you've performed the puja?' he wanted to know.

Apparently, in my horoscope, all the seven planets of Vedic astrology – Sun, Moon, Mars, Venus, Jupiter, Saturn and Mercury – were sandwiched between *Rahu,* the moon's north node, and *Ketu*, the moon's south node. Even those with just a passing knowledge of astrology knew that the villainous Rahu and Ketu were the Teja and Gogo of the planetary system, out to wreak havoc on your horoscope. A grim search on Google revealed '*Kaal* means death. A person born under the kaal sarp yog passes through death-like agonies throughout his life.' Amongst the numerous ill effects listed – and there were so many that it made me wonder how I had gone through life all these years without being hit by a bus – was the one that seemed to plague my love life. My efforts were not meant to yield desired results. In the nanosecond before I began to seriously hyperventilate, I was relieved the delay in my marriage wasn't my fault after all. Having established that, I turned all manner of anxious and fearful – *Shit. Shit. Shit. Now what? Would I never find someone? And if I did find him, would it not last? I didn't say I wanted to move to Italy. I may have been open to it. But not permanently! Just until love found me or until my parents found love for me! And in any case, I may have just thought it, I never actually said it!*

As it turned out, the degree at which the planets were positioned in my horoscope meant that my kaal sarp dosh wasn't very severe.

'You must perform a kaal sarp shanti puja to mitigate the effect of the yog,' advised the pandit.

'Let's do it,' said my Dad.

'You could do it in Mumbai...' said the pandit pausing for effect, 'but at the holy Shiva temple at Trimbakeshwar you will get the best results.'

As if the ritual was like an out curl blow-dry, you could do it at home, but for best results you had better go to the parlour. 'In fact,' he continued, 'I know just the guy...'

And so it was that I found myself at 5 a.m. on a chilly Wednesday morning with my big toe immersed in the holy Godavari river, wondering if that constituted a dip. Apparently, Wednesday was the day the gods on the kaal sarp committee met, which explained why there were hundreds of people in various stages of undress, either about to wade into the water or on their way out, with whatever garment they'd held on to clinging to their soaked, shivering bodies at the Trimbakeshwar complex that day. The holy water – and I am writing this on a Sunday in the hope that the kaal sarp god committee is on a break and my remarks will go unnoticed – was a horrifying, infectious-skin-disease-giving shade of murky brown. My mother and father were already in, waist deep, trying very hard to look nonchalant about it – the things Indian parents will do to get their daughters married. I think the last time they gave me such fake smiles must've been when I was a kid and they were luring me into my paediatrician's examination room for tetanus shots. I took a deep breath and thought of all the reasons I wanted to get married.

To begin with, there was the wedding trousseau. You're probably judging me right now, but it's bloody hard to hold off on those gorgeous silk and chiffon saris with their backless brocade blouses and delicate zardozi borders just because you can't find a guy with the right sense of humour. Give a girl some bridal magazines and enough me-time at the parlour and the thought may, eventually, cross her mind. Frankly, if you think about it, you'll agree that people have gotten married for far less than the exquisite set of gold jadau jewellery my Mum had purchased expressly as my wedding gift. I am just saying. Then, there was the home I wanted to decorate. I had this vision of myself sashaying about an impeccable white apartment, hosting a party with unpronounceable finger food. I'd flit from one guest to another making sparkling conversation, with a witticism here and there about why NaMo or why not NaMo or whatever it was the glitterati was fixating on that week. Since no party worth its salt is any success without a handsome man lurking by your side, his hand on the small of your back, ready to headbutt any guy who so much as glances at you, I wanted to find myself a husband ASAP.

And before all my feminist friends get on the phone with each other to fix a time and place where they can burn me at the stake, people, just take a moment to picture me at that party – without a man. All my married friends would be whispering amongst themselves – *Such a beautiful apartment and nobody to share it with, the poor thing. We should really set her up with someone. How about Amit? Oh, didn't he marry that hot radio jockey? Do we know anyone else? Ashutosh? No, he lost his job and his apartment since his divorce. And last I heard, he has become p-r-e-t-t-y fond of the bottle. So what? She doesn't need his apartment, she has this one. Let's at least suggest him to her.* Do you really want that for me? Do you?

I could go on about why I wanted to get married, but that day, on the banks of the Godavari river, I had gotten only so far as the honeymoon I wanted to go on, the tandem bicycle I secretly wanted to ride and the pictures of it I so badly wanted to post on Facebook, when the water began to seem harmless after all. I waded in bravely and took a swift dip before speeding back to the changing quarters to scrub myself clean with a bar of Lux soap.

Now that we were most likely infected, we were considered cleansed, at least in mind and soul. So we donned new, straight-out-of-the-shopping-bag kind of new, clothes and began the kaal sarp puja. From what I understood, this would be a six-hour-long ritual that involved invoking and appeasing various gods starting with the residing deity of the temple, the Lord Mrityunjay Trimbakeshwar. In the next five hours we'd be reaching out to Lord Shiva, Lord Ganesha, Goddess Durga, the god of water, the gods of the nine planets, the god of time, the Golden Serpents – basically at least one-third of the vast pantheon of Hindu gods. It seemed like it was going to be a power-packed yagna. I was glad that we were getting in touch with so many gods and goddesses because that increased the probability of at least one of them paying attention to my little problem and feeling benevolent enough to sneeze on it. We'd just made the requisite ten donations and were well into the first part of the yagna when the pandit pointed to a pot of water in front of us and indicated that each of us were to take a sip from it.

'It is powerful water . . . from the river Godavari,' he said.

I stared at him paralysed.

He took my inaction to mean that maybe I didn't understand him.

'Holy water ... we collect it from the river. You had the bath today morning, right?'

Yes, right? Exactly, right! We had a bath in it. So did some 600 other people. And that's just today. So what was it you wanted us to do again?

*

If the Hindu arranged marriage system were the Italian mafia, then astrology would be its godfather. People rarely ever contemplated marrying without its consent. From the age you began your hunt, to the person you finally picked, to the precise time of your wedding ceremony, you sought its blessings every step of the way. Biodatas sent out into the world could be vague about a lot of things but you didn't mess with the date, time and place of birth. Those were mentioned right on top, unfailingly and accurately, so that before any actual contact was established, both sides could have birth charts drawn up, studied and matched. Arranged marriages were risky enough without ignoring birth charts and inviting the wrath of the godfather. While there were dozens of theories on which horoscopes could be deemed compatible to each other, the one thing all the theories agreed on was that matching them was a must. By comparing the angles of the planets in the solar system and their position in the zodiac at the time of the individual's birth, astrologers could predict not only the longevity of the proposed union, but also its quality. Through mathematical calculations, astrologers claimed they could infer an individual's temperament, intelligence, health, sexual drive, financial aspects, reproductive capability and spiritual development, and on that basis they could predict whether the two people in question were suitable for each other and whether the relationship resulting from their union would be a harmonious, balanced and successful one.

And if astrology was the godfather – I swear I'll drop the analogy at some point, but I am really on a roll right now – then the fiery, red planet, Mars, was its right-hand man, its most formidable henchman. The presence of a strong Mangal – that's what Mars went by – in the 1st, 2nd, 4th, 7th, 8th or 12th house of the ascendant chart – pretty much anywhere on your horoscope – was a thing to be noted and feared. You didn't marry someone with a Mangal unless you had a strong one in your chart too – that was the decree and astrologers predicted terrible outcomes for those who disregarded it. From disharmony in the marriage to a flagging career and financial troubles to even death, there were dire consequences for those who crossed Mangal. Unless, of course, you paid up the protection fee. The manglik – the person with Mars in the horoscope – could perform a puja, wear a recommended gemstone, and if she really had her heart set on marrying a non-manglik, she could trick Mars by first marrying a banana tree instead. By naming the unsuspecting banana or peepal tree as your spouse, you managed to direct Mars's attentions towards the said tree, while you sneakily married the non-manglik of your choice. It was all very cloak-and-dagger, and people choosing to get married the arranged way seldom bothered to meet a person whose status on Mars was different from theirs. In fact, it was a common belief that those with a strong Mars either married very late in life or very early. I have a thirty-five-year-old cousin, a pretty and intelligent girl, who has been meeting men the arranged way since she was twenty-three. She hasn't kept count, but if I were to estimate one guy a month – and that's a very conservative number – she must have met about 120 men so far.

There's no reasonable explanation as to why she is still not married despite having had the inclination as well as the opportunity to do so, except the strong Mars in her horoscope.

The astrologers are so confident and so all-knowing about their business that you either had to have a death wish or be madly in love to go against their advice.

However, things changed about a year after my kaal sarp puja, when I ended up at loggerheads with the godfather. I was almost twenty-six now and still single. Frankly, both conditions were surprising because that meant that I had lived to become a year older despite drinking numerous sips of that terrifying 'holy' water and that, in spite of drinking it, I was still single. But I was finally in the middle of what felt like it could be the real thing. You remember Samit, the guy I shared my umbrella with and how we met several times, and then met his parents and never heard from them after? Well, during the time we were waiting to hear back – before I had asked my father to find out – I became very nervous with the silence at the other end. Things had gone so well at the last meeting that I was actually surprised we weren't at the printers already selecting a card for the wedding. One day at work, unable to bear the suspense and getting nervous enough to lose five consecutive games of Scrabble with random 'easy' level people online, I took matters into my own hands. No, I didn't pick up the phone and call him – what was I? Desperate? No. I decided to pay a visit to a tarot card reader instead. She was supposed to be quite the expert. Her services featured regularly in the *Bombay Times*, so there was no doubt that she knew her stuff.

'So Meeti, how can I help you?' she wanted to know, once I was settled in front of her.

'Well ... there is this guy...'

She smiled knowingly. What else was a twenty-something-old girl doing at a tarot reader's in the middle of the day? She shuffled her cards and asked me to touch one before proceeding to lay them out on the table between us.

'You've drawn the magician,' she said, studying my love-life spread, 'extremely gifted and powerful but not always what he seems.'

'Okay,' I said, wide-eyed.

'Give me his name and birth details. Also, do you have a picture?'

'Yes!'

Now, before you begin to think that I was so besotted that I had taken to carrying his picture around, you forget we live in the age of social media, so all I had to do was direct her to his Facebook page.

'Hmm,' she said, 'interesting,' while she studied him in his blue T-shirt standing against the Mediterranean sea, then in another window, she fed his birth date, time and place into a horoscope software and drew up his birth chart on her computer.

'There seems to be a delay.'

I nodded frantically, forgetting that it was I who had told her a few minutes ago that we'd been waiting for their answer.

'There's a woman in a position of power who's causing him to hesitate. Maybe his mother?'

Yes, now that I thought about it, maybe his mother hadn't liked me as much as I thought she did.

'But don't worry,' she said studying his picture again, 'it will pass soon. This is meant to happen.'

She studied his horoscope and then mine.

'Ask someone to intervene, some common connection. In any case, it must happen ... sooner or later.'

If words could really be like music to the ears, this was a Beethoven symphony but it was a pity you couldn't dance to it, because I would've done the Macarena all the way home.

Since you know how that story ended, you can understand why I decided I would never kiss the godfather's ring again. No tarot. No palmistry. No readings of any other body parts, thank you very much. But as it turned out, I had spoken too soon.

THE HAND THAT ROCKS THE CRADLE

You know that scene in the movies, the one at the hospital when a brand-new mum and dad are staring at their sleeping, day-old baby through a glass window, all teary-eyed and smiley-faced at the same time? I have this theory that that is exactly when Indian parents first start planning their children's weddings. I am not exaggerating. While other parents may be turning into puddles of mush over their baby's tiny, curled-up fists or pixie ears, I am almost certain that Indian mothers are gazing at their little wrinkled angels and imagining which of their friends' little angels they can set them up with. While Indian fathers are imagining the day their little girl gets into a long white car bedecked with flowers and gazes at them through the window sobbing inconsolably before driving off into the sunset and living happily ever after.

When my Mum read the opening paragraph of this chapter, she rolled her eyes and asked me to stop watching so many movies. But I swear, it's true. Indian parents take the business of getting their children married at least as seriously as the Shiv Sena takes the safekeeping of everybody's morals. It is right on top of their KRA. If there were an appraisal form for Indian parent performance, way above those middle-class Indian staples like 'Feeding offspring till said offspring is about to burst', 'Making offspring doctor or engineer or – but what else is there?' and 'Instilling fear of God in offspring so offspring can never refuse prasad', would be, in a bold, drum roll kind of font: 'Bagging suitable match for offspring'. If you scored well on that one, you were set, you would be considered to have officially arrived. It didn't matter then that you got an 'F minus minus' on things like 'Cultivating civic sense in offspring so that they don't treat the city like a private urinal'. Society would nevertheless congratulate you, promote you and give you a whole new set of additional responsibilities like 'Conducting yourself like an in-law' or 'Getting on offspring's case to have offspring', which you would undoubtedly enjoy far more than the ones before.

When she read this part, my Mum told me to just

wait until I became a mother. As if the act of pushing a baby out messed up not only your nether regions, but also the part of your brain responsible for rational thought. Because, really, where's the logic in MARRIED OFFSPRING = SUCCESSFUL PARENTS? So your child now has an official permit to procreate, congratulations, but how is that a reflection of your parenting skills? Your child has also, most likely, acquired a set of in-laws, a joint bank account and a home loan. Still, how does that make you a good parent?

There's really no reasonable explanation as to why marriage assumes an importance of such elephantine proportions in the head of Indian parents. Of course, I can hardly complain, I probably would not be married at all if my Mum hadn't made it her life's work to set me up with a never-ending string of suitable men for the two and a half years that it took me to find my husband. She approached the task with such single-minded zeal that it would've made Mrs Bennet look like a slacker. During that time, it was her job to spread the word amongst friends and relatives that they were looking for a boy for me, and also to chat up random acquaintances who she may have bumped into at a mall or a movie theatre, and bring the conversation around somehow, with great dexterity so that it looked like it had come up naturally, to the topic of eligible bachelors. I am not sure how she actually did it. What must that conversation have been like?

At a mall:

Random aunty (RA) 1: What a great sale, right?

Mum: Yeah, did you check out Vero Moda?

RA 1: No, is it any good?

Mum: Yeah, in fact, you should totally bring – *insert name of Random aunty's daughter* – along, lots of things for that age. How is she, by the way?

RA 1: She just completed her MBA at yada yada yada...

Mum: That's great!

RA 1: How about Meeti?

Bingo!

Mum: She is doing well ... working with a multinational advertising agency. In fact, we've started to look for boys for her ... so if you...

RA 1: Oh, actually ... there is someone I may know...

Mission accomplished.

At a restaurant:

Mum: Fancy bumping into you here!

RA 2: Oh, how good to see you!

Mum: I see even you've left the kids at home!

RA 2: Oh, they are too cool to have dinner with their parents now!

Mum: Yeah, we've been through that age with ours as well. What are they up to now?

RA 2: Both of them are studying medicine ... yada yada yada ... How about yours?

Quick mental jig!

Mum: My son is in his last year of engineering, but my daughter has finished her studies ... working at an advertising agency now. In fact, we've just started to see boys for her.

RA 2: Oh, good to know, good to know. I'll keep that in mind.

Mission accomplished.

But I wish I could say that that was all she'd had to do – just let people know that we were looking and a bevy of beautiful men had magically appeared at our doorstep.

A – I wasn't much of a catch. Opinionated, vocal and career oriented, I wasn't the sweet – read handleable – daughter-in-law that most Gujarati mothers imagined for their sons.

And B – I think, during my let's call them husband-seeking years, the proportion of eligible boys to girls was as skewed and desperate as Mumbai's people-to-apartment ratio. For every ten Gujarati girls of marriageable age there seemed to be one available guy. And if you were picky enough to want a boy who could string a complete sentence in English, it dropped down to one is to twenty. And if – jeez, really, is it a wonder you took so long to get married? – you also wanted him to be at least half a foot taller than you, well then you'd best bring along a searchlight. And yet, despite the odds, I had forty first meetings – which meant that my Mum found forty single men in the right age, education, caste and income brackets – all looking to get married. And that's not even counting the ones I spoke to on the phone nor the ones I refused to go meet because I didn't like the font they'd used in their biodata – I'm only kidding of course, I hated the font *and* the colour of the ink. It was a number that required sheer resourcefulness and perseverance. In fact, it was a little like when you started your own business – yeah, I know it sounds kind of funny, but really – it wasn't enough to just let friends and relatives know that you'd become, say, a Tupperware agent, you had to network with the right people, you had to advertise in the right places, you had to cold call, pitch and even do some product placement.

My Mum, think adorable Type A person with a perpetual sugar rush, went about the business of getting me married with the focus of a finalist on *The Apprentice*. She called up friends she hadn't spoken to in years for 'I-passed-by-that-park-we-used-to-love-and-just had-to-call-you' type of completely fabricated chats, she subscribed to different newspapers to look for advertisements in their matrimonial sections, she got herself a yahoo account, mastered the email and learnt how to switch on the computer – exactly in that order – so that she didn't have to wait around for me to mail people my biodata and see if they'd reverted. She composed and placed her own classified ads in newspapers, visited matchmaking bureaus and rifled through hundreds of '1978 to 1982' biodatas to pick a few which I could go through and decide if I wanted to meet, and always a believer in the power of 'top of mind', she dragged me to weddings and other dressy occasions, so that I was 'visible' at my prettiest – as I had said, product placement. In any case, this kind of campaigning meant that almost every other Sunday, I was either exchanging biodatas with someone, talking on the phone with them or going to meet them. If it was taking me a while to find a husband, it was never because of lack of choice.

And still, that's not all that she'd had to do. When she took up the task of arranging my marriage, I doubt my Mum realized just how intense her new job would be or how her new profile would involve essaying any number of different roles depending on the need of the hour.

EVANGELIST

Now, I always knew my Mum was proud of me, but during those husband-seeking years when I heard her talk me up to random acquaintances, I had to actually resist the urge to look behind and double check that it was indeed me she was speaking about. She was like a passionate brand evangelist. Everything about brand 'Meeti' was spectacular – from where brand 'Meeti' worked, to where she holidayed, to where she got her haircut was not only worth mentioning but also worth writing a jingle about. From the pineapple-nougat cake I perfected to the handbags I designed and sold in my free time to the award I won for my advertising work, all the high points of those years were brought up frequently and opportunely – sometimes in a direct manner, sometimes covertly and at other times by proxy, meaning, she made my Dad mention it. It was a pity that sending out year-end holiday cards with family photos and updates was not an Indian tradition – how my Mum would've loved the medium. It would've been such a perfect showcase for my many talents and achievements, real and imagined. In fact, had I mentioned it to her that there was in fact such a custom in the West, she'd have gone right ahead and started one amongst the Gujaratis. What's more, it would've picked up and become quite a hit, because as we all know, Gujaratis will try anything new as long as it is 'cool' and vegetarian. So completely devoted was she to brand 'Meeti' that if I were a fairness cream, the company would've tripled its brand recall, doubled its sales and been inclined to fire its advertising agency, marketing consultant and the PR firm, because its brand evangelist, my Mum, had not only taken over all three roles, but was also, as was her wont, doing them better than they'd ever been done before.

Looking back, I am surprised it didn't mess with my brother's self-esteem or at least cause some nasty sibling rivalry – because in those days, to hear my Mum talk, people would've been surprised to learn that she had a son at all.

STYLIST

Now, I may have given the impression that my Mum's chief occupation was finding suitable spouses for her two children. But in reality, my Mum is a fashion designer, and a successful one at that. This, combined with the fact that my Dad is a textile trader, made the subject of clothes a very important one in our house. We were the kind of people who didn't buy new clothes because we had a dinner to go to, we made dinner plans *because* we had new clothes we wanted to wear. If we were trying to be economical, we'd go to that dinner and order one starter instead of two or split the dessert into four and the cola in two, but it would always be in something new. I suppose my brother would object to being clubbed with us, seeing that he is a boy and that's what boys who like large, black T-shirts with skeletons on them are supposed to do, but he was an equal participant in our little, post-mall ritual. Any time one of us went out and bought new clothes, no matter that it may have been in the company of each other, we would come home, try them on again and parade around in them for the benefit of everyone at home. In fact, the first time I realized that this was not a wide-spread practice was after I was married and my husband wanted to know why I was trying on a dress again which we'd just purchased together that day. *You mean, I should just put it in the cupboard? Like, straight out of the shopping bag? As is? Without even checking to see if it looks as good in our home mirror as it looked in the trial room? Are you serious?*

It was hardly surprising then that my Mum and I gave the question of what I should wear for my first meeting the kind of time and consideration that the Hollywood people reserve for their ensembles on the Oscars' red carpet. Arranged marriages depended heavily on first impressions. Which meant, my outfit had to convey exactly who I was – a young woman who fell neatly in between two extremes: the cigarette-touting-beer-chugging advertising professional and the home-science-degree-flaunting Gujarati girl. It had to not only suggest that I was career oriented but also that I had held on to my traditional values. And it had to make me look thin. Now you may remember, I wasn't fat. *You do remember that bit, right?* But like many curvy Gujarati women, I have the kind of childbearing hips, the sight of which can immediately cheer up bleary-eyed gynaecologists about to put their scrubs on for a 2 a.m. delivery. It was a delicate brief and to tackle it my Mum called upon that great boon to the pear-shaped Indian figure, the kurti. For those of you unacquainted with a kurti, this is a diabolically clever article of clothing which you wear as a top with a pair of jeans. It can be thigh-length or knee-length, snug or flaring, sleeveless or full-sleeved and low-necked or buttoned. Basically, it is so versatile and so flattering that it is as if the gods were trying to make it up to Indian women for sticking them with Indian men.

Over the course of my boy-seeing years, Mum designed so many kurtis for me that slowly I gathered a Sunday-boy-meeting collection that could rival a debutante's wardrobe for a season at court.

THERAPIST

Had my Mum realized what a complex job profile she'd have when she took up the task of arranging my marriage, she'd probably have negotiated the terms better: say, twenty boys, two years, shortlist five, pick one, let's go, go, go. But she had just been so grateful that I'd finally agreed to delegate, that she'd accepted the position without even asking for any back-end support. Sure, my Dad was around when she needed to play good cop bad cop. But 'handling' me wasn't always that simple.

I had only agreed to an arranged marriage in theory, without really understanding the tediousness the process involved. Which meant that every so often, after watching a soulful, romantic film or reading a particularly introspective travel story or coming home from an exceptionally dull coffee, I'd hold forth on the subject of love or begin to enumerate the many obvious joys of the single life and announce that I would never go for a meeting again. How then to get me to go for one that very afternoon? It required an ingenious mix of philosophy, persuasion and patience. And yes, blackmail.

Some days, when I was feeling dejected about how long this was taking, she'd speak to me about karma. She believed that life was what you made of it, but there were three certainties for everyone – *janam, maran* and *lagn* – when you were born, when you died and whom you married. These three events were fixed and all you could do was keep hunting and bide your time. 'It will happen when it is meant to,' she'd say often and with conviction.

On other days, when I was reluctant to go meet someone because their biodata wasn't up to the mark or because their picture wasn't appealing enough, she'd warn me on the perils of judging too hastily. 'You won't know until you go,' she'd say with a sort of ringing finality. I don't know about you, but I find it pretty hard to resist advice that actually rhymes – somehow, it just feels more truthful.

However, on the off chance that I didn't fall for it, she had another approach. She'd show me two biodatas, the first one would be blah, like cleans-and-organizes-his-sock-drawer-in-free-time kind of blah and she knew I'd reject it in a heartbeat. Then she'd whip out the second one, the one she had wanted me to consider in the first place, and say with a long-suffering sigh, 'Fine, how about *this,* then?' Having so blatantly rejected the first one, I'd be forced, for the sake of appearing reasonable, to agree to a meeting or at least a phone conversation. *Now, I've actually studied psychology for four years. I know there is a name for what she was up to. It's another matter that I can't, for the life of me, remember it right now, but the point is that in spite of being well versed in the art of negotiation, I almost always stepped right into her little trap. She was good at her job, my mother.*

Very often though, her modus operandi would be to just hear me out. I'd rant and vent and when I was done, she'd agree with me. 'Yes, it's pretty awful. You don't want to do it? Fine, let's just forget about it.' Then for a few weeks she would let me be. And one day over a Sunday lunch, she'd mention causally that there was this interesting biodata that had come to her and she could pass it along if I wanted to glance at it. Usually, by then, I'd have cooled off enough to grunt, 'Fine.' Besides, when you've spent enough Sundays meeting guys, you kind of start missing it if too much time goes by and you haven't had a chance to tell anyone exactly where you saw yourself five years from now. *Of course, I realize just how lame that sounds. What do you think?*

There were times though, when none of my Mum's pop psychology worked. Like when I had finally, finally, met someone I wanted to meet a second time and they said no. No amount of rationalizing or philosophizing could put a positive spin on it. It sucked. Period. And I was damned if I would put myself through that again. It was in such extreme instances, that Mum would show her full hand and play the 'For me, beta?' card. It was like the ace of spades, it trumped all. The thing was, Mum was usually a tough cookie, so when she got all teary-eyed and emotional and asked you to do her a favour, it was so unsettling that you just did it. You went and met the next boy in the line-up. Which meant that instead of brooding about what went wrong, you put on something nice and consumed a lot of caffeine. Which in turn meant that you cheered up. And come next Sunday, you weren't as reluctant to continue on your quest.

My Mum is hardly the only parent to have treated the task of getting her daughter married as seriously as the Muslims take the business of going on Hajj. Most parents feel equally 'obligated' to see their offspring settled in their lifetime. From preparing and dispersing their children's biodatas to making the first exploratory calls and conducting the background checks to accompanying them on meetings, managing their matrimonial accounts, screening the incoming requests and even saying no for them, they are involved in every step.

Sometimes, however, one of them may go a step too far. A friend of mine once met a girl who he'd been chatting online with for a couple of weeks. As their meeting progressed, he began to get the distinct feeling that she didn't remember much of what they had spoken about previously. A little annoyed at having to constantly repeat himself, he finally asked her if she'd been chatting with many other people and if that was why she couldn't recollect the particulars of their conversation. Imagine his surprise when she assured him that she never chatted with anybody and that he may have spoken to her mother who chatted with prospective suitors from time to time, to ensure that the ones her daughter finally met were suitable for her. *Yes, I know. Pretty f***ed up.*

I suppose you can't blame parents for being overly zealous about the task at hand, seeing as they have their entire sense of self-worth riding on their ability to get their children settled, but sometimes in their enthusiasm, they hinder rather than help their cause. A cousin of mine once spoke to a mother, who after agreeing to send her elder daughter's biodata to him, inquired whether she could send her younger daughter's work résumé as well. My cousin worked for Citi and her daughter was looking for a related job. *Yes, you guessed it, she killed exactly zero birds with her stone.*

I think I finally get why Indian parents throw such lavish weddings. If you worked that hard to win a pitch, you'd party too.

GROOM WANTED FOR TWENTY-FIVE-YEAR-OLD, 5 ft 7 in. GUJARATI GIRL

When a year had gone by and they still hadn't found a suitable match for me, my parents realized they'd have to step things up a notch. The traditional mode of spreading the word – relatives, friends and the three ladies who played bridge with our neighbour every Tuesday – had yielded unsatisfactory results. I had met a few unexciting men, the kind they wrote the 'Enjoy aamras in Amsterdam and patra in Paris ads' for. I was beginning to see where the Gujaratis got their reputation from. Our community spent big money, the highest in the country in fact, on travel, but very often, we left our spirit of adventure behind. I was beginning to get disillusioned. It seemed to me that I wasn't going to find my type of guy amongst the diamond merchants and cloth traders my family was introducing me to. To keep me interested, my parents figured they'd have to widen the net.

MATRIMONIAL BUREAUS

To understand how a Gujarati matrimonial bureau is run, it is essential to understand the Gujarati women who run it. To begin with, they have a keen entrepreneurial bent of mind. Like their male counterparts, the idea of running a business and turning a profit thrills them. Add to that the fact that the Gujaratis are an affluent community. Which means that in the absence of the 'need' to join the workforce and bring home a pay packet, the women have most likely stayed at home to look after their kitchens and raise their children. Which in turn means that they are dying, like *daaaayeeeeng*, for some real action. Add to that the fact that many may now be finally retired. Meaning, they have acquired daughters-in-law to worry about what goes into young Jignesh's dabba, and thus, freed from the demands of managing a battalion of servants and orchestrating grand meals three times a day, they now have ample free time on their hands. Finally, top that with the other minor detail – they are women, playing cupid is second nature – and you have an insight into the minds that run the matrimonial bureaus.

The bureaus are typically run from the homes of one

of the founding members. The women assemble there a couple of times a week in the afternoons, post lunch and siesta, to organize their files and meet prospective clients. But that is not where their real work happens. To understand how they function, think of them as an elite clique of aggressive investment bankers. They are smooth. They are extremely well networked and they can sniff a potential merger even on holiday on a different continent. They are also always working. A glimpse of a young woman at a temple, an introduction to someone's aunt at a wedding, a snippet of conversation overheard at a funeral or the mere mention of an eligible man at the beauty salon, their antenna is always up and tuned to the remotest possibility of a new deal.

The way to enlist their services was simple. You, meaning the mother of the girl/boy, turned up at the home of one of the founders on the time and day they'd suggested, with a copy of your girl/boy's biodata and a recent photograph for the registration process. This involved filling up a form and paying up a registration fee, in exchange for which they filed your child's biodata in an age-appropriate, caste-appropriate and area-appropriate file. Then on the basis of that biodata, and of course, your child's general attractiveness, they gave you a select number of suitable biodatas of the opposite sex. You went home with the details of, say, five boys, whom your daughter could meet that month, as well as the promise of your daughter's biodata being passed along to the mothers of suitable boys who were registered at the bureau. If things worked out, you called the bureau people with the good news and asked them to take your daughter's biodata out of circulation, and if they didn't, you went back next month and got details of five new boys and so on.

The first time my mother registered me with a bureau, she paid a fee of ₹10,000 and brought back about half a dozen biodatas. Some of those guys I met, while in some cases the horoscopes didn't match. The majority of them, however, were either studying or working in the US – that great El Dorado of the Gujarati community. 'Let me take down your details,' the boy's mother would say on the phone, 'and once Bhadresh is down in December, we will get in touch to set up a meeting.'

Very often, Christmas would come and go without any word from Bhadresh, and we began to suspect that this had not been his idea in the first place. His parents had proactively registered him with the bureau, and then come December, the heavily jetlagged Bhadresh had taken one look at the pile of biodatas in the living room and thrown a fit. 'Ma, I told you not this time!' he'd yell, or 'Ma, I told you I am seeing Jenna! And I really, really love her!' 'But at least go meet Jigna once,' his mother would plead helplessly, thrusting the photograph of her best-looking find in his face, terrified at the prospect of a white, meat-eating daughter-in-law. Then Bhadresh would stomp away in disgust and shut himself up in his room. And his poor mother would ask Ganpat, their trusty household help, to take the four-course meal she'd prepared in anticipation of Bhadresh's arrival – who'd expressly told her that he wouldn't be having dinner, since he was landing at 2 a.m. – to his room and hope that he wouldn't refuse that as well.

As you can see, this is a scenario I have given a lot of thought to because it would really rankle me that my Mum would have to call them again in December and check if Bhadresh was down and be told that he had 'postponed his trip'. This happened to us no less than four times, after which my Mum told the ladies at the bureau to not give us the US boys because I think it finally struck her – maybe because I had said it to her some two dozen times by then – that even if Bhadresh's mum had called, her own daughter would've refused to go for the meeting, since I had no intention of going to the US on a dependent visa and playing house for some guy named Bhadresh.

After a few months, once we'd exhausted this bureau's quota of 'Jain, 1978 to 1982, postgraduate, at least 5 ft 10 in. tall' men, we moved to another bureau in another part of south Mumbai and repeated the process. This time, the registration fee was ₹15,000. As I put down these numbers, it is beginning to seem to me that the cost of getting me married – and I am not counting the expense of my wedding here – might have paid for that writer's retreat in Italy.

In retrospect, I really should've just gone, seeing as how hanging about in Mumbai was making no difference in the greater scheme of things. Despite the resourcefulness of the bureau women and their proclivity to close a deal, I wouldn't be married for another year and a half.

MATRIMONIAL WEBSITES

I suspect that before my parents asked me if I would consider putting my profile up on a matrimonial website, they must have argued between themselves about who would bell the cat. It was a dangerous expedition, because as they'd expected, I threw a gargantuan fit. *What's that now? A matrimonial website? So you guys have just given up on me?* – Please don't look for logic in this line of thought – *Why not just give an ad in the papers. Or better, just put up a few hoardings across the city! You know what? I don't even want to get married! I don't know why I agreed to let you set me up in the first place. It has caused me nothing but heartburn! Heartache! I mean heartache! You think this is funny? Actually, it is! My life is a joke! So not only am I such a loser that my parents have to find me a husband, we now have to broadcast the fact on the World Wide Web? What do you mean overreacting? I know WHAT it MEANS! Thank you very much!*

As usual, my Mum was stuck with the task. So one evening, she slipped it in ever so casually during dinner, that one of her new clients – a girl whose trousseau she was designing – had found her husband through Jeevansathi.com and that she was all praises for the portal.

In retrospect, I can't believe how incredibly convenient it was that my mother managed to find a 'new client' whenever she wanted to introduce a new, potentially difficult idea to any of us. She had a new client whose son fainted after a twelve-hour stint at a video game parlour around the same time that she was trying to get my brother to stop wasting his time on Counter Strike and focus on his CET. There was a new client whose husband had started to go for walks following a cardiac scare when she was trying to convince my father to take up his yoga again. And now, here was this new client with the Jeevansathi success story.

'Okay, here's the deal,' my mother said after I had calmed down enough to suspiciously inquire how long it had taken her client to find the husband. 'We won't put up a profile for you just yet. First, we'll just log on to the website and see what kind of guys there are. Then, if you say that you want to give it a shot, you can write your own profile. How about it?' she asked.

Always a sucker for control, this was an enticing proposal. Plus, my curiosity had been piqued. If there was a way to get married without the whole circus routine of the traditional arranged marriage, I wanted to know.

At the time, there were just a handful of well-regarded matrimonial websites out there. My Mum and I opened up Shaadi.com, Jeevansathi.com and BharatMatrimony.com in three separate windows – even if we were just window-shopping, we would, as was our wont, be thorough – and settled in for an evening of checking out potential husbands while sipping steaming cups of chai. If they ever made an Indian version of *Sex and the City*, this is exactly the kind of scene you'd find in it.

At first glance, there seemed to be many advantages to signing up:

a. These were matrimonial websites, so it followed that the men featured there must be serious about getting married.
b. There were a variety of advance filters already in place. If you were hunting for a tall, lean and geeky banker, all you had to do was simply ask for one. There were check boxes with a range of educational qualifications, occupation profiles and body types. You just ticked the qualities you wanted, like you were ordering a pizza – *large, thin crust and extra cheese, please* – and presto, there they were, piping hot and up for grabs. Okay, so I may have exaggerated the piping hot bit, since this is Indian men we are talking about, but you get the gist.
c. All the awkward questions had already been asked and answered. Say, for instance, you wanted to marry a smoker so that the two of you could step out into the balcony post dinner and share a Lucky Strike or two under the moon. There was really no way to ask the nice young man Aunty Patel set you up with if he enjoyed the occasional cigarette without giving it away to him and to Aunty Patel *and* to all of Aunty Patel's

kitty friends, CWFW – Club of Women for Women – friends, Tirupati temple friends, weight-watching friends and subsequently, your own parents, that you were (gasp) a smoker. On the matrimonial websites, however, all you had to do was tick the 'Smokes' box in the relative privacy of your own office cubicle and a range of smoking men – does that sound like I mean hot men? I really need to choose my words more carefully, what I meant was men who smoke – turned up on your screen, who were, in addition, tall, lean and geeky bankers.

Or let's assume you wanted to know – and everyone always wants to know, so don't even pretend otherwise – how much a guy made last year. There was absolutely no way to ask that question upfront without coming across as a scheming, money-minded shrew – even if the guy didn't think it, you might rest assured that Aunty Patel and her cronies would promptly decide that you were after money and go to town with the news. In any case, even if Aunty Patel wasn't part of the equation, say, you'd been set up by friends, this was still a supremely graceless question to ask. So how then to ascertain whether the guy could afford to send your future kids to Harvard for undergrad? In a traditional arranged set-up, you'd probably be stuck for the better part of your meeting trying to gauge the guy's lifestyle by making note of things like the car he arrived in, the cellphone he used and where he went on holiday the year before. Which seemed to be pretty inefficient when compared with the matrimonial websites, which did away with the need for deduction games by providing a simple and straightforward 'Annual Income' box. Problem solved.

d. The traditional arranged marriage mechanisms had a short radius. Your family friends, relatives and the bureau women, all functioned within their own social circles that were defined by geography and economics – which meant that pickings could often be limited. A friend of mine, who'd been meeting girls for a long time, actually met the same girl twice in a span of three years – he didn't realize he'd met her before, until he was almost halfway into the conversation and felt a strange sense of déjà vu when the girl began talking about her younger sisters. With matrimonial websites, the world was your hunting ground. When I fed in my search criteria, it was with great glee that I observed a large number of six-feet-tall Jain men turn up in London – the city I had always believed I had a karmic connection with.

e. It made great reading. I mean just listen to this stuff:
   1. *I am smart, handsome and take no bullshit*. If nothing else, I'd definitely give this guy a job writing bumper stickers.
   2. *I am a simple but bold, honest, hard-working, romantic, attractive, independent person.* I'd actually like to meet someone who thinks this highly of himself. I can't

think of any quality that he missed out on, except maybe modest?

3. *Mom is a housewife, a lovely lady to talk to and a wonderful mother. Dad is retired.* If this isn't Oedipus complex, what is?
4. *In human society, males are protectors, females are nourishers. So you can be assured as a potential husband I have the ability to protect my family ... My mom tells me she started to play* ghar ghar *with all her sahelis at the age of ten. All little girls were playing ghar ghar together with those Barbie kitchen sets. I understand the importance of marriage and will put my best effort to work out compatibility with the shortlisted matches.* Can you even imagine a meeting between Sheryl Sandberg and this guy?

   Sheryl: I really think we need more women to lean into their careers and to be really dedicated to staying in the workforce.

   Guy: Sweetie, it is my job to work and make sure you have everything you need. Your job is to give me babies who look just like you.

   Sheryl: You know, it's hard to believe this when you are young, but a husband who does the laundry is more romantic as you turn older.

   Guy: Relax, baby, you are not listening to what I'm saying, I'll get you a maid to do the laundry.

Needless to say, I signed up. Not only did I put up a picture with a personal profile – where I waxed eloquent about my zest for life, my love for literature and my chronic wanderlust – so that the guys featured there could get in touch with me, but I also paid a neat little sum to get a three-month membership, which allowed *me* to contact them. After three months had passed, I renewed the membership for another quarter. At the end of those three months, I deleted my profile from the site and washed my hands off the entire affair. I had ended up meeting exactly one guy in all this time, which led me to a few conclusions:

a. The money would have been so much better spent as a contribution to my writers retreat fund.
b. Despite the fact that these were matrimonial websites, there were plenty of men out there who wanted to 'do fraandsheep first and marriage later' which was essentially code for, *I just want to hook up but the hot girls at the nightclubs treat me like I have measles, mumps and conjunctivitis, all together – which, by the way, actually happened to me one fun summer – so this is where I spend my Saturday nights.*
c. There were also men out there who didn't know that they were out there. Enthusiastic, computer-savvy parents had created their accounts and written up their profiles. They responded to the queries their son's pictures received, as well as got in touch with the women they thought their sons would appreciate, and exchanged details and pleasantries before letting on that they were doing it on behalf of their offspring.

Some even made liberal use of the 'chat' options on the portals, and I thought that, subconsciously, they actually enjoyed the process. As though after thirty years of being married to the same person, they had a chance at a do-over. It was a cynical theory but I could easily picture it – a retired dad staying up late at night to check out pictures and profiles of young women, supposedly for his son. It was such a liberating excuse that it must have felt like getting permission to watch porn for medical reasons.

d. All the awkward questions had indeed been asked and answered, but that didn't mean that the answers were always truthful. Human beings have an innate need to present the best version of themselves to the world. You may safely assume that while making my profile if I'd been asked to enter my weight, I'd have lied. Not significantly, but yes, deliberately. Out of sheer vanity, I'd have put it down as a couple of kilos lower than it really was. So it didn't surprise me that some men looked older or plumper in the 'recent' pictures they eventually sent, when their profiles on the portals seemed to suggest otherwise. Also, the 'Annual Income' box turned out to be a bit of a lame duck. The income brackets chosen often seemed to be disproportionate to the occupation and the position that had been listed. I suppose men being men, treated the question as if they'd been asked how far they could pee – they exaggerated.

e. Sure, the world was your hunting ground. But unless you could find some common connection who could assure you otherwise, there was always a possibility that your six-feet-tall Jayesh Mehta from London was actually James Moriarty in disguise.
f. It *was* fun reading, but after a while the terrible grammar just got to you.

MATRIMONIAL ADS

When I reached marriageable age – my parents don't seem to remember the exact year, but knowing my father, it is entirely possible that this happened while I was still in college – my parents, like most Gujarati parents, began to subscribe to one of the two largest Gujarati newspapers in the country – the *Gujarat Samachar.* Every Wednesday morning, in thousands of Gujarati households, fathers picked up the *Gujarat Samachar* and turned the pages to the classifieds section with the kind of eager anticipation they usually reserved solely for the stock pages. Other men may turn straight to the sports section, but Gujarati men were less into games that prescribed dribble-block-pass, and more into the kind that involved buy-hold-sell. The Indian cricket team may have tanked the evening before, but the only performance that could move Gujarati men to tears was that of their beloved *shers* – shares. At Gujarati breakfast tables, stock potential was discussed so frequently and at such length that Gujarati women were as aware of the share prices of Infosys and Reliance Industries as that of onions. On Wednesday mornings, however, the focus of the conversation at our house changed – this was the day the paper featured eligible Gujarati boys and girls looking to get married. My parents sat at the breakfast table, pen in hand, highlighting appropriate ads like fresh graduates circling 'Wanted' positions.

'See this one,' my Dad would say, '5 ft 11 in., Jain, twenty-eight-year-old architect.'

My Mum's eyes would twinkle.

'From Wadala,' he'd add.

My Mum would wrinkle her nose. An architect was awesome. In fact, I suspect she had a thing for architects. But the middle-class suburb of Wadala, not so much. She would sigh and take down the details anyways – she had her priorities sorted, my Mum.

'This one's twenty-seven years and Malabar Hill,' Dad would continue.

'But?' Mum would ask, sensing there was a catch.

'Diamond market.'

'Hmph.' My Mum would sigh again.

Guys who worked in the diamond market, as we were increasingly discovering, were not always well educated. They entered the family business young, while still in college, and spent years learning how to sort, grade and value and, eventually, buy and sell diamonds. Theirs was a small, tight-knit world, where formal degrees were superfluous and exposure was limited. However, there was sometimes a possibility that the guy had spent some time abroad, pursuing courses at the Gemology Institute of America or had developed a broader horizon because he travelled frequently to foreign trade festivals and interacted with international clients. And on that off chance, my Mum would take the details down.

'What else?' Mum would ask.

'That's it,' Dad would say, scanning the page, 'unless we want to look outside the community…' – by which he meant Gujarati but not Jain.

Mum would raise an eyebrow speculatively and they would ask the cook for second cups of tea. All this while I finished breakfast and left for work.

After her list for the day was done, Mum would spend the afternoon making calls, getting email IDs, exchanging biodatas and if everything checked out, setting up a meeting or two. If not, she'd wait for Saturday.

On Saturdays, the other large Gujarati newspaper, *Janmabhoomi*, ran its own set of classifieds. My Nani, who subscribed to that paper, had taken it upon herself to comb through them finely and report to my Mum with her findings on Saturday afternoons.

'Take it down,' she would urge Mum, '5 ft 7 in., twenty-eight years and works for a bank.'

'Meeti is 5 ft 7 in.' Mum would protest on my behalf.

'Can't we ask her to not wear heels?' Nani would ask innocently.

Because surely, as long as we could trick the guy into thinking that he and I were well matched, what possible hesitation could I have? Rather than explain to her that I felt as passionately about tall men as she felt about her collection of organza saris, Mum would just jot down the details.

When almost two years had gone by without any success, my parents decided that the time had come to publish a matrimonial ad of our own. By then, I'd made my peace with the methods my parents were employing to get me married. In fact, in a rare bout of maturity, I even offered to help them.

'Why don't I write it?' I asked, what with me being a copywriter and all, it was only natural that I was assigned the job of making my own ad.

'No,' said Mum, almost instantly. 'You stay out of it. You got to write that matrimonial profile, didn't you?'

She said it as though the way I had written my profile had been responsible for my lack of success on the matrimonial websites. Which is complete hogwash because I thought I'd done a brilliant job with it. I could've picked a fight with her right then and there, but I was being mature those days, so I let it go.

'Fine, you do it,' I said, breezily.

So one fine Wednesday morning, the following ad appeared in the Mumbai edition of the *Gujarat Samachar*:

ALLIANCE INVITED FOR 25-YEAR-OLD GUJARATI JAIN GIRL. BEAUTIFUL AND TALL, 5ft 7in. FROM WELL-SETTLED, SOUTH MUMBAI FAMILY, WORKING AS COPYWRITER IN REPUTED MNC. PARENTS OF SUITABLE BOYS REQUESTED TO GET IN TOUCH AT 98211***.**

It was succinct, I had to give them that. I suppose when you were paying by the word – extra, in fact, to print in bold – you made every word count. I giggled when I saw it. 'Beautiful? Who says things like that? This is as bad as those guys who describe themselves as "tall, dark and handsome"!'

My mother rolled her eyes and settled herself next to the phone. Did I mention that we'd acquired a new phone number for the express purpose of getting me married? Much earlier, when they had just started looking, Mum felt that it was just easier to give a separate number to the parents of prospective grooms than the one she gave her clients, tailors and embroidery artists. 'That way, I will be sure to return calls,' she had said, only half joking. We got about six calls in response to the ad – out of which one was from one of the bureau ladies trying to acquire new business. Though I must say that this wasn't a statement on the quality of the ad. The ratio of marriageable girls to guys continued to remain disproportionately skewed. There was just no getting around it.

One of the first callers wanted to know if I had a CA or an equivalent degree.

'She's got an MA,' said my mother.

'Oh ... even an MBA or a CFA would've done,' said the guy's mother sounding genuinely disappointed.

'She's got a master's in English Literature,' my mother reiterated, immediately irked. My mother was proud of her children's education – she'd sent my brother and me to the best schools in the city and encouraged us to pursue our passions. My brother was a computer engineer while I was a writer, and my parents had supported both choices equally. Now here was this woman implying that her daughter's qualifications were as fictional as the subject they were in.

'My son is a CA. We really wanted someone...'

'Yeah, yeah, that's too bad,' said my mother and hung up on her.

Ironically, with another caller, things swung in the opposite direction.

'But he is doing so well for himself!' protested the guy's mother when Mum told her that I wasn't meeting men who weren't at least college graduates. 'You know,' said the guy's mother – in that tone that people use when they want you to know that you're making the biggest mistake of your life and they can't wait for the day they can gleefully wag a finger and say, 'I told you so' – 'he has been running our family business for five years now.'

My mother apologized to her sincerely. There was nothing else to do. In a country where college education was cheap and readily available, to not have a bachelor's degree was an aberration that was difficult to overlook. Of course, there was always the possibility that when I passed up on a meeting with a college dropout I was saying no to the next Bill Gates, but somehow it seemed like a chance I should take.

With the next caller, everything checked out. He was 6 ft 2 in. with a master's in chemical engineering and lived in the right part of the city. My Mum exchanged email IDs with his mother and just as she was about to hang up, she asked, 'What year was he born in?' Turned out he was ten years older than me.

'That's a huge age gap!' she said, surprised.

'Oh, don't worry, we are completely okay with that,' said the guy's mother.

My Mum declined politely and promptly called me at work to rant. 'Can you believe the nerve of some people! Of course *she'd* be okay! But why would *we* get our daughter married to a guy who is a decade older? Things haven't come to that!'

It was sweet of my mother to say so, but at twenty-five, from where I stood, things were beginning to seem pretty grim. What next, I wondered? Community events?

Manan had attended a matrimonial event organized by members of his community to get young people of marriageable age to mingle with each other. He said it had been pretty intense. People had shown up in large numbers. Almost all candidates had been accompanied by a set of parents and a sibling or cousin or two.

'When you entered, you got a token number that you had to wear through the evening,' he said, 'as well as a topic you had to speak on.'

'What do you mean speak on?' I had asked incredulously.

'Meaning, for the topic or against the topic, like I was given "Should women work post marriage", someone else got "Love marriage versus arranged marriage".'

Had I been paying complete attention, I'd have been outraged that people were still discussing whether women should have a career. But I was trying to wrap my head around this newest mating ritual.

'So there was like a group discussion?'

'Not a group discussion ... it was more like a speech.'

'Like with a mike and all?'

'Yeah, they called out your token number and then you went up and introduced yourself and spoke for a few minutes.'

'And if the opposite sex liked your "public speaking", they took down your token number?'

'Yeah, and then during the course of the evening, the organizers would announce that token number so-and-so had requested to speak with token number XYZ. Then both parties would step up and go to a corner to have a little tête-à-tête.'

'Jesus,' I said, shuddering. It sounded like an awful cross between speed dating and an elocution competition.

'It sucked,' Manan agreed, 'but of course, after that there was a delicious buffet dinner,' he said with twinkling eyes.

'Of course,' I said, since no Gujarati event could even be contemplated if it didn't involve at least one elaborate meal, 'not to mention the fact that you met your future wife there.'

'Yeah, that too,' he said, grinning.

I suppose I should mention at this point that I finally met my future husband through a matrimonial ad. It wasn't this one, and it wasn't for another six months, but at least I didn't have to attend one of these community events, and for that, I guess, I should be grateful.

'NO' – HOW TO SAY IT, HOW TO TAKE IT

'They want to meet again,' Dad said, as soon as he'd hung up the phone.

'That's nice ... right?' ventured my mother, looking at me expectantly.

I scrunched my nose and shook my head.

'Why not?' my Dad demanded.

'Just ... no.' I knew it was a vague answer but I really didn't have a good reason.

The guy, a chartered accountant, had been smart and sensible and we'd had an easy enough conversation, but there hadn't been any chemistry. Granted, it was an arranged date, which took place at my house, in my parents' bedroom no less – I sat on the bed and he, on an armchair – while our parents and a pair of relatives discussed the benefits of kapalbhati in the living room outside. And looking for 'chemistry' in that kind of setting was about as futile as waiting for an adrenaline rush in a needlepoint class, but I had gotten good at sensing potential and picking up on even a hint of a spark. I could tell that with this guy, there was none. Not that I had any intention of even trying to explain the concept to my father. Because this is more or less how it would go:

Me: Daddy, there was no chemistry.

Dad *(stares at me blankly)*

Me: *(trying again)* There was no spark, Daddy.

Dad: *(turning to my mother, with an expression of 'What in the world is she on about now?')*

Me: *(exasperated)* There was no attraction, Daddy!'

Dad: *(embarrassed)* Is that my phone ringing? Yes, that's my phone ringing. *(Makes quick exit)*

So I just shrugged.

'They are going to ask as well, you know,' he said, referring to the relatives who'd arranged this meeting.

'I don't know, Dad ... we didn't click, okay?'

'Click! What does that even mean? I can't go about telling people Meeti didn't think she "clicked" with the guy. They'll never show us any boys again!'

I looked at my mother imploringly.

'Are you sure, you don't want to give it another go?' she asked me.

I nodded vigorously.

'Okay … let's just tell them the horoscopes didn't match,' she said, brokering a temporary peace.

Rejection after a date – whether you're at the receiving end or the one saying no – is always rough, but it was plain crappy with arranged meetings because at any given time there were at least half a dozen additional people involved. Your parents, his parents, relatives, neighbours or family friends in the know, the ladies of the bureaus and any other members of the family who tagged along – were all not only privy to the decision but, surprisingly often, instrumental in making it. People didn't just set you up and then forget all about it – they wanted a low-down on how the meeting had gone, they wanted the gory details and if they had an opinion on who you should spend the rest of your life with, they were not shy to express it. Not only did that make saying 'no' hard, because you had to explain to that many people what exactly you meant when you said you didn't 'click', but being rejected was acutely more painful because everyone involved found out you had been turned down.

People close to me tell me that I have a rather robust sense of self-esteem. It's the kind that allows you to automatically assume that when the boss calls you into his office for a chat, it must be because he wants to commend your good work. Or if a woman is staring at you, to suppose that she must like what you're wearing and wants to know where you picked it up from. It rarely ever occurs to me that maybe she is looking at the lipstick stain on my teeth. But the thing is that, while it may appear that I am self-assured, people often don't realize that this is more than anything else an elaborate coping mechanism. An ingenious way to manage my gigantic need for approval. I have such an astonishingly great need for people to like me that if I didn't think they approved in the first place, I don't think I could function at all. I swear, it is so debilitating to always be concerned with people's opinion of you that I think, subconsciously, I've just conditioned myself to assume they think well. Because if they didn't, then oh boy, would we have a problem. I find it almost impossible to let such things go, to just shrug like a normal person and tell myself, 'Oh well, you can't please everybody.' No, that would be too wise and uncomplicated. I have to obsess and fret about it, and invest a significant amount of energy in wondering how to win their approval. Which is pretty time-consuming, not to mention crazy. So I deal with it by believing, and I mean really, really believing – you can't fake-believe this stuff – that of course they like me, because, come now, what's not to like?

When you take someone with my kind of mental make-up and put them through the arranged marriage process, you can cause so much damage that a mystery – apparently, the collective noun for doctors and other medical professionals is 'mystery'. I know, how could I not use it, right? – of shrinks could live off their whole lives from the proceeds of the sessions it may take me to recover.

Let me explain.

To begin with, you've in any case started out feeling a bit like an underdog because contrary to how you expected your life to turn out, you have had to accept that you may not find a suitable husband on your own and you've had to enlist the help of your parents. Then you bump into a school friend (SF) on the train and you have this conversation:

Me: So how are things?

SF: Good. Things are good. I am off to Rome next week.

Me: Ooh, nice! Holiday?

SF: Holiday-cum-wedding. You remember Namrata *(another classmate)*, right? She is getting married to an Italian.

Me: *(staring at her silently while urging my mind to stop paying attention and quickly go hide in its happy place)*

SF: *(continuing, oblivious)* They met each other while studying in New York and now they are getting married in this beautiful little Italian church. It's all very romantic, and he's soooo cute!

Me: *(almost faint with the effort of keeping myself from jumping off the train)* How lovely, how lovely…

When you compare your school friend's life with your own, that is, you go to her Facebook page and pore over pictures of her with her beau, you feel as awesome about yourself as Vivek Oberoi might at Cannes. But, say, you get over it. Say, you tell yourself such is life and display all kinds of maturity. Do the Arranged Marriage Gods reward you? Do they say, 'Now that this damsel has put her faith in us, let us get her a husband, pronto?' No, that would be too boring. When would they have their share of fun? So they devise an elaborate test for you, much like a devious video game with obstacles and difficulty levels and everything else. As you can probably tell, I haven't played too many video games – only Super Mario to be honest, and that too, never till the end – but I have spent enough time lurking behind my brother's shoulder, waiting for him to get off the computer, to understand the basic format. Your alter ego starts off on a mission. At each stage of the journey, it encounters all sorts of crazy hurdles. More often than not, it takes a sound pummelling. If it proves resilient enough to survive till the end, it wins the prize. Correct? Well, the arranged marriage process is pretty much like that. Let me give you an example of Difficulty Level 4. Here's a conversation I had with another school friend – yeah, I don't know why I bother to talk to these girls.

Me: *(calling up school friend – SF2 – to check how her first arranged meeting had gone)* Soooooo? How was it?

SF2: *(sounding unreasonably upbeat)* Not bad. Not bad at all.

Me: *(not the answer I had expected, seeing as this was her first)* Go on, tell me more.

SF2: Well ... it was pretty good, we really hit it off. We are going ahead with it.

Me: *(genuinely uncomprehending)* Going ahead with what?

SF2: You know, getting engaged.

Me: *(silent)*

SF2: Hello?

Me: *(spluttering)* You are kidding, right?!

SF2: No. He seemed pretty sorted.

Me: *(still in shock)* You've only met once!

SF2: *(shyly)* Twice, actually ... last evening went so well, we decided to meet for breakfast again.

Me: Once! Twice! Same thing! What are your parents saying?

SF2: Oh, they loved him and his family!

Me: *(still unable to wrap my head around this, needing very much to lie down)* Oh my God ... this is crazy. Congratulations!

Summary of Level 4:

Challenge: Your friend finds a husband within days of beginning her arranged marriage process, while you've already toiled for over a year.

Task: To go to Level 5, you must not only attend this friend's wedding but also boogie at her sangeet like you are a contestant on *So You Think You Can Dance*.

As you proceed ahead in the game, you sense the arch villain, the great red-eyed monster, Rejection, looming in the background. You must battle with it eventually, but already you can see flashes of it and you can tell that the actual encounter will not be pretty.

Here's a Level 6 situation:

'Any word?' I asked my Mum, a day after I had come back from one of my arranged meetings.

'Not yet. Should we call?' Mum asked.

'Absolutely not,' I said instantly.

'You know he wasn't bad...'

'I am not interested, Mom ... just curious,' I said, interrupting.

'Fine.'

'Anything?' I asked the day after.

My Mum shook her head.

'Hmph.'

Out of the forty men I met, I had pleasant meetings with more than two dozen of them. It was a different thing that I didn't come away from any of them thinking, 'Hmm ... that was nice', but as far as the conversation was concerned, it had been smooth enough. Which is why it really, really bothered me when we didn't hear back from them.

'Were you going to marry him?' Shilpi would ask me bluntly every time I went to her all downcast.

'No,' I'd say truthfully.

'Did you want to meet a second time?'

'No,' I'd say, honestly again.

'So, why do you care?'

'I don't know, I don't know!'

It was surprisingly deflating, this silence at the other end. I wasn't expecting every guy I met to hurry home and declare to his parents that he'd marry me or stay single for the rest of his life, but I had taken it for granted that people would at least want to meet me again. Their lack of interest wasn't affecting my ego as much as my sanity. I tortured myself by imagining the conversation these guys had when they went home from a meeting with me.

'How was it?' the guy's mother would ask.

'All right.'

'Do you want to meet again?'

'Naah ... she was too intimidating / career oriented / modern / outspoken / tall.'

'What do you think they go home and say?' I would ask Manan, who always refused to be drawn into this particular conversation.

'You know, there are plenty of men you don't call back,' he would say, or something equally sensible but useless.

He just didn't seem to get the point, that guy.

Of course, this was nothing compared to how utterly devastated I was when someone I *had* liked turned me down. Fortunately for those people in my life who had to deal with me on a daily basis, this didn't happen more than a couple of times, because if I'd been insecure before, I became insufferable then. Take, for instance, the time I met the XLRI graduate who worked with a media company. We'd had a fun and lively coffee date that lasted over an hour. So when Mum asked me, like she always did, if I wanted to meet him again, I quickly agreed.

'He is travelling for work,' said his mother, when my Mum called her to set up another date. 'He'll be back in a couple of days, I'll call you then.'

'He just got engaged,' she said, when my Mum called to follow up a week later.

Apparently, he'd met this girl several times before he'd met me. He had liked her then, but he'd continued meeting other girls since things were still undecided between them.

'Brilliant,' I said, when I heard, before locking myself up in my room.

It seemed to me that regardless of what level I was at, someone had set the difficulty level to 'hard' by default. Not only was I smarting from having been turned down – that damage would probably need some hypnotherapy to undo – but I was also amazed at my colossal bad luck. After almost eighteen months of looking, I'd found one guy who I wanted to meet again – and he had gone and promptly gotten hitched to someone else. It was as if the Arranged Marriage Gods had to go attend an All Gods Town Hall and had been forced to delegate the running of my video game to some minor demon.

On the heels of this meeting, a friend of my Mum's set me up with Nishant – the most been-there-done-that diamond merchant I'd ever met. He lived in the US where he was pursuing his MBA, after which he planned on joining his father's jewellery business. This coffee date was even more fun than the one with the XLRI guy. 'Aah,' I told myself, 'so this was what the gods had planned for me.' When we parted, we exchanged email IDs so we could keep in touch. He was going off to the US that week but he would be back in a few months, when we planned on meeting again. I went home in good spirits and promptly wrote him a long email – I find it really difficult to write any other kind – the week after. I never heard back.

'Maybe he is still jetlagged,' suggested Shilpi.

'Maybe he got busy with his studies,' said Manan.

'Give him some time to settle down,' said my Mum.

So I gave it a rest for a few days, until I saw him online.

'Hi!' I typed out on chat.

I waited for a few seconds for him to answer. When he didn't, I continued, 'How is it being back?'

After a long time, I got a reply, 'Hi, this is not Nishant. This is his brother.'

'Oh okay ... well, tell him I said Hi.' I wrote back.

And that wasn't the last of it. If anticlimax was an art form, my life had perfected it. A few weeks later, when my mother met her friend who'd set us up, she learnt that he had just met me because his parents had insisted and that he wasn't really looking to get married.

'Brilliant,' I said, when I heard, and promptly shut myself up in my room again.

I wasn't sulking each time I holed myself up in my room like that. Well, maybe just a little bit, but what I really did was chant. Those days, I repeated the mystic Buddhist mantra Nam Myoho Renge Kyo like the world was ending and this was my secret code to get aboard Noah's ark. On a plain piece of paper, I had put down a few goals, starting with the one about finding a suitable husband along with a list of qualities that I wanted him to have.

TALL
FUNNY
SMART
PASSIONATE
HIGHLY EDUCATED
WELL TRAVELLED
RICH
ROMANTIC
POWERFUL

Yes, I am perfectly aware that I sound like I read too many Mills & Boon novels, but these were genuinely all the things on my list. I didn't see why I had to lower my expectations and make things convenient for the Arranged Marriage Gods – it wasn't like they were returning the favour.

I'd sit cross-legged on my bed while I chanted with this piece of paper in front of me, trying to visualize the kind of person I wanted to be with. For 'Smart' I had given him glasses and for 'Rich' he got a shiny, black car, but I always found it difficult to picture 'Funny'. I tried giving him one of those T-shirts with jokes on them but it didn't seem to fit, maybe because I liked guys to dress sharp. In any case, I held the essence of this guy in my heart and fervently, night after night, asked the Universe to please, please send him to me. The Universe showed me the finger instead. It arranged for me to meet and get turned down by Samit.

'I didn't like him in the first place,' said Manan, when he found out what had happened.

'Yeah, me neither!' said Shilpi.

'Why didn't you say anything earlier?' I demanded.

'You seemed excited and we didn't have a good reason ... just a not-so-good feeling,' said Shilpi.

They insisted they weren't just being loyal. But I didn't care, I was beginning to suspect that there was a glitch in the video game I was playing, the coding seemed flawed and the hurdles, insurmountable. I'd hit rock bottom and the only way to scrape back to the top, it seemed to me, was to have an affair. It wasn't the smartest recourse but it was really the Universe's fault – it had whipped up a timely candidate and delivered him conveniently to the cubicle right next to mine.

Moody and talented, Kay was my new art partner, and we'd quickly become friends. But lately, he seemed to have developed a thing for me. He would sit beside me while I played that great addictive guzzler of all my time and free will, Word Twist, and cheer me on for hours on end. He'd leave Five Stars on my desk after lunch, once he learnt that it was my favourite chocolate. He'd insist on dropping me home when we worked late nights even though he lived on the opposite side of town. He asked me out for movies on an almost weekly basis, in spite of being repeatedly turned down. For my bruised and battered ego, spending time with him was like receiving essential first aid at a crash site. I was tempted to have some fun.

'Why not?' said Shilpi, 'Give it a go…'

'Don't even think about it,' said Manan.

It was like the Gamemasters – I wasn't sure who was in charge any more, the Arranged Marriage Gods or the wayward demon – had devised a grim challenge round, and then gone ahead and offered me a cheat code.

I didn't take the cheat code because what I did take was a fateful weekend getaway. On this trip, I got hopelessly lost in a forest as dark as a coal mine and was convinced I'd never make it out alive. It's an interesting story but this isn't the place for it. The only reason I mention it is because while I floundered up one wrong trail after another, certain that I was going to be seized by a wild leopard, I did some soul searching. I reflected on life and my seemingly endless quest to find a husband, and I decided that if the Universe managed to get me out of here in one piece, I would never doubt it again. I'd trust that it had a plan for me and continue doing what I knew I should – meeting men with an open mind and a willing heart.

*

A few pointers on handling rejection – all far easier said than done, of course.

1. Believe that there is something better out there for you. Somehow, there usually always is.
2. In no situation does the old 'It's not you, it's him' apply as soundly as in the arranged marriage scenario. When you don't hear back from someone after an arranged meeting, the chances are pretty high that it really was not because of you. There could be as many reasons as there are people involved for why that phone call doesn't come. I once met an architect who'd recently lost his father. He seemed like a great guy and our meeting was going swimmingly well until we came to the subject of his Dad, at which point he got a little emotional and teary-eyed. Still, when we parted, he said, 'It was really nice meeting you' – and I knew he meant it. But they never called back for a second meeting. My guess is that he was still grieving and not really ready for an important decision like marriage. Point is, don't take it personally.
3. 'I think she is being too picky,' declared Savita aunty, my Mum's friend. She was telling us about her niece

who she'd recently tried to set up with a friend's son. Her niece, who lived in town, had rejected the guy's biodata because he stayed in the very distant suburb of Thane.

'I mean, you have to compromise somewhere,' she continued, looking at my mother for confirmation.

Mum nodded, while at the same time giving me a wry grin. We too had turned people down for similar reasons before. In a huge and expensive metro like Mumbai, your address was a fair indicator of your socio-economic background. In the arranged marriage situation, when you were looking for someone with a similar lifestyle to yours, it was reasonable to want to stick to certain areas of the city. But there was no point in explaining that to Savita aunty, or to any other aunty for that matter.

An arranged meeting, even if it is just between the girl and the guy, is never a private event. By its very nature, it requires the cooperation of a number of people. And when people get involved, there is bound to be talk. From who you met and what you wore to what you ordered and why you were refused. Everybody has a view on everything. You can't control what people are going to say. What you can do, though, is not let them affect you. *Yes, I know. But sometimes, the best advice is obvious.*

4. If you are the one doing the rejecting, be unfailingly kind. Even if it means that you can't be honest. Say,

you want to turn someone down because they seem duller than dishwater. I'd say keep that evaluation to yourself. In the hands of the aunty brigade, it can only hurt the chap's prospects further.

Here are a few true rejection stories that should make your own difficulties with the subject seem as breezy as a PG Wodehouse book:

1. When my friend Reshma turned a guy down, she received a full-page email from him. 'Some people have all the pain and some people have all the luck,' he wrote, and told her about now difficult his life had been, how he lived with a stepmother because his own mother had died and now she'd just added to his misery by rejecting him. 'You should be slapped, you've broken someone's heart,' he finished. 'We had spoken for less than ten minutes,' said a flabbergasted Reshma of her first and only meeting with him.
2. My friend Trupti told me of a guy with whom she thought things were going rather well. They'd already met a couple of times and were contemplating taking things ahead, when she brought her friend along for their next meeting. They chatted briefly, shared a few stories about Trupti, after which her friend left.

   'He seemed so sweet!' she called to tell Trupti the next day. 'You should totally go for it.'

   'I am so sorry,' he called to tell her an hour later, 'but I really liked your friend.'

3. Trupti – thank God, the girl has a sense of humour – has another story about being turned down by a guy and his family who told the middle person that they had assumed 'the girl would be at least as fair as her mother' – they'd seen her mother elsewhere. *I know you want their address so that you can send them hate mail and maybe even a horse's head. But my editor says it's not a good idea to put it in the book.** Besides, you know what's worse than the fact that they think like that? That they actually said it out loud. They didn't think they needed to make an excuse, they were not embarrassed, it was perfectly acceptable to just come right out and say it. We are so never getting over our white-skin complex.

* *You can write to me about it though, if you like.*

HOLD YOUR NOSE AND JUMP

It was a balmy Sunday morning in August and I was in high spirits. I was supposed to meet Hemant, a well-spoken hotelier with whom I had already had two interesting phone conversations. For a Gujarati boy, hotel management was an unconventional choice of career and Hemant had already won brownie points for being different. Besides, never had I found common ground with someone so instantly – we both loved to travel. His job required him to visit different cities across the world for extended periods of time; he enjoyed it and for my part, seeing that I had always wanted to be a travel writer, it was like someone had taken my idea of a perfect life, gift wrapped it and left it at my doorstep. We were to meet that evening and I was looking forward to it, but first, I had to get out of the other meeting my Mum had set up for that morning.

'Why in the world did you set up two meetings on the same day?' I asked my Mum.

'I know, I know … Hemant's was fixed a week ago, but the other guy, Maulik, is going back to the States next week.'

'Yes, but why am I meeting the other guy in the first place? You know I don't want to move to the US.'

'His brother says he plans on moving back soon.'

'And what if he changes his mind? People do that, you know. I don't want to be stuck thousands of miles away from friends and family forever, and that too on a dependent visa! Besides, I didn't like his picture.'

'What's wrong with it?'

'I don't like the haircut.'

'Oh, come on now!' said my Mum. 'Just go meet him once, you can talk to him about his plans for the future and you can see that haircut in person. Maybe it looks better now? His profile seems excellent, MBA, investment banking … and his brother was really nice to speak to.'

'Oh, now that's a new reason to get married to someone … "His brother was nice to speak to". How compelling!' I said angrily.

'You know what? Don't go. Just pick up the phone and cancel it yourself,' said my Mum, equally angry.

We continued to quarrel about it some more, until my brother stepped in to negotiate. It was finally agreed that I'd go for a short while. My brother would drive me to the coffee shop, run a few errands in the area, then phone me when he was done and I'd make my excuses and leave. Which is why he was a little surprised when he called me about half an hour into my meeting asking if I was ready to go, and I said, 'No, you carry on, I'll be a while.' He couldn't have known that I already had an inkling that I'd finally met the man I was going to marry.

Friends, both those who view the arranged marriage process with the distance, fear and fascination that one usually reserves for dangerous circus acts, as well as those who stand at its periphery like you'd stand on the edge of a pool with one toe immersed in the water to see how chilly it is before diving in, never fail to ask me one question – 'How does one decide?' What about a few meetings can possibly convince you to spend the rest of your life with someone? What if you make a mistake? What if it's too late by then? What if you've already rejected the person you were meant to be with? What if you say 'yes' too soon and the right guy is still out there? How do you know? HOW DOES ONE DECIDE? It all really adds up to that. All those other important choices you have to make along the way – who you meet, what you ask them, what you tell them about yourself, why you reject them – seem like mere trifles in front of the gargantuan 'How does one decide?'

When I began my hunt for a husband, I'd decided to tackle the question with 'time'. I had not one, but two friends who'd married the first guy their parents had set them up with and continued to remain happily married years later. While I envied them their serendipitous marriages, I knew that I wasn't okay with that kind of quick decisiveness. I had planned on meeting any guy I was considering seriously, as many number of times as I thought necessary. It was contrary to how the traditional arranged process usually worked, but I'd enlisted my parents' support on this point at the very beginning. It could take months or even a year, but I wasn't going to take up a second surname until I hadn't gotten a good, long look into his soul. And yet, I agreed to marry Maulik within a week of meeting him. It was highly uncharacteristic, especially for someone who has been known to dither over a pair of shoes.

To understand this brave, newfound readiness, I've replayed that Sunday afternoon and the events of that week in my head many times.

The first thing I noticed when I met Maulik was that the haircut had grown out nicely after all. Instead of the unfortunate-looking crew cut in the picture, he now had a full head of neat salt and pepper hair with a few wayward cowlicks standing up whimsically, giving his bespectacled, serious-looking face a kind of contrasting boyish charm. A couple of inches over six feet, he was lean and dressed in a bright yellow polo T-shirt and jeans.

'I am so sorry,' I said, apologizing for having gotten late – my Mum and I hadn't realized how long we had fought – 'the traffic was awful.'

'That's all right,' he must have said, 'no harm done.'

I have no recollection of what he actually said because I was struck by two separate observations at the exact same time:

1. He spoke 'normally'. I'd met guys visiting from the US before and very often, regardless of how long they'd actually stayed abroad, they had acquired such a strong accent and they clung to it so diligently that it seemed they were more attached to it than to their beloved H1 visas, which allowed them into America in the first place. Maulik had been in the US for the last six years but refreshingly, his speech seemed unaffected.
2. His voice was so deep that listening to him was like finding yourself on the most profound page of *The Unbearable Lightness of Being*.

It seems to me that I am giving the impression that it was love at first sight. Let me be clear – it wasn't. We weren't young enough or naïve enough for those sort of easy explanations. Besides, our parents had set us up. There's only so much enthusiasm you can muster for a date that your mum seemed more excited about. And yet, our conversation had a remarkably natural rhythm. He told me about his life in New York and described the long hours, the short deadlines and the adrenaline rush of his job as an investment banker on Wall Street. I spoke of client briefs, creative blocks and the business of ideas and described the pitches, parties and presentations that were such a staple of my advertising job in Mumbai. He told me about the chilly, glittering, white winter mornings of Buffalo, where he'd gone to business school, and of the warm, lifelong friendships he'd formed there, and I spoke of how we'd discussed Plath and Plato over hot cups of oversweet Nescafe in college, while the rain poured outside our terrace classrooms, gently spraying the pages of our books, teasing us to look out the window and dream lush green dreams. We spoke of our travels. He had funny stories about misadventures with food in China, while I was still giddy from my recent trip to France.

'We, my friend and I, stayed with a local lady in Paris and learnt how to make plum jam,' I gushed.

'That sounds wonderful,' he said.

'It was ... I also got to practise my French.'

'You speak French? I can give speeches in French,' he said in a mock boast.

'Really?' I said, grinning.

'Well, one in any case ... I gave it at a farewell assembly in school. I was so nervous and I memorized it so thoroughly that I think I still remember it.'

'Let's hear it,' I said.

'What? Here?'

'Why not?'

'No, I...'

'Come on.'

Grinning, he entwined his hands in front of him in the classic choir boy pose, and gave me a look, as if to say, 'You asked for it', and began, '*Respectez President, Monsieur Pinto, notre Directrice, mes professeurs et mes cheres amis, je vous remercier pour me donner l'occasion de parler avant vous. C'est un adieu partie à dixieme class et je suis sûr pour portez deuce memories et ils conseille est prouver être a bon citizen. Remercie.*'

As I leaned back into my chair, smiling, listening to the worst French I'd ever heard, a funny thing happened, he suddenly began to seem very familiar. It was as if I'd known him for years and, now, we were just catching up after a long break. A sense of calm fell over me then, and it occurred to me that I had finally met the man I'd marry. I couldn't be sure, but the thought had just ambled into my head, settled in comfortably and seemed very much at home. There was no accompanying storm of nervous voices, doubts and fears – just a quiet, inexplicable, yet pleasant stillness in my stomach. It was very different from anything I had experienced before.

We ordered a third round of coffee and continued talking for a couple of hours more. Then, because it was obvious that we had plenty more to say to each other, he asked me if I wanted to meet again and I said, 'Yes, I'd like that.'

'Four hours?' said my brother, as soon as I entered the house.

I grinned. My parents were sitting in the living room with an expectant look on their faces.

'It was going well, he seemed really nice,' I said to them, explaining why I had taken so long. 'We are meeting again ... tomorrow.'

My parents seemed surprised – this hadn't followed the circuitous arranged marriage route for second meetings – but pleased. They knew better than to ask me more. Experience had taught them that talking at length about a meeting just raised all our expectations, and often for naught. Besides, we didn't have much time.

'You have to meet Hemant soon. Why don't you change and freshen up?' said my Mum.

I have no idea when my meeting with the hotelier had slipped so completely out of my mind.

'Can we cancel it?' I asked her, quietly.

This wasn't my usual whiny, I-hate-my-life attempt at getting out of a meeting and salvaging my Sunday. That conversation would involve a volley of protests from my side and all kinds of negotiation manoeuvres on the part of my mother, until one of us, usually her, exhausted the other into submission. But this time, I think she sensed something in my tone.

'Are you sure you want to?' she asked me. 'You were really looking forward to it.'

'I know ... but I just want to focus on this one thing right now.'

And that was the end of it. There was no further

discussion. I was left to dwell at leisure on the day that had passed and to plan other important things, like what I'd wear for my coffee date with Maulik the following day.

The next evening, toppled over by our enthusiasm, coffee spilled into dinner. We chatted late into the night about our plans for the future. He loved his work and believed that Asia was where the action would be in the coming years. He wanted to settle in India and build a life for himself amongst his large extended family. I didn't love advertising as much as I enjoyed it. I wanted to explore writing in all its other forms. I wanted a life where life itself was at least as important as deadlines. We talked about our friends and I told him about the vital, as-important-as-salt kind of role they played in my life. We spoke about the books we'd read, the music we enjoyed, and how much we both loved *The Dark Knight*, *Seinfeld* and Aamir Khan. Then, we decided to meet again.

On our third date, he showed up with a box of dark chocolate truffles.

'I went to a bakery while waiting for you,' he said, as he handed it over to me.

The modern arranged marriage was rarely spontaneous, let alone romantic. His gesture, while it wasn't much, made me smile all evening. He was leaving for the US in a few days and we decided we'd stay in touch through email.

'I can make another trip to Mumbai in November and we'll see how we feel then,' he suggested.

'Perfect,' I agreed. Three months was enough time to gain a deeper understanding of each other and to decide if ours had just been a momentary meeting of minds or if there were enough conversations between us to form the beginning of a lifelong relationship.

And yet when I returned home that night, I did something inexplicable. I called Manan who was holidaying in Ladakh and asked him if he could come home two days sooner.

'Why? What for?' he demanded, surprised.

'Just tell me you will try,' I said, and not a word more, hanging up as soon as he had promised he would.

Next, I proceeded to call Shilpi and asked her if she'd join Maulik and me for lunch the following day.

It was a strange whim but I wanted both my best friends to meet Maulik before he left for the US. In retrospect, my actions amaze me. Hadn't we just said that we'd give ourselves three months before we decided one way or the other? What, then, was the point of this rash behaviour? What would I achieve by having Manan cut short his holiday? I had known Maulik for precisely three days. Had life still not managed to teach me the virtue of biding my time? Our parents hadn't even met yet. What if they hated each other? Hadn't I seen enough parents become deal breakers? What if he went back to the US and disappeared on me – surely, I remembered what that felt like? What if I was so fed up of the entire process that I was simply jumping at the first decent guy

I liked, who liked me back? These were all legitimate doubts, which should have been amplified by my ever-ready, ever-fecund imagination and tormented me, but none of them even occurred to me that night. I slept as peacefully as a fat Brahmin snoozing after a huge, free Sunday meal.

The lunch with Shilpi went off well, and then it was time to meet the parents. They lived in Vashi, a very distant suburb, and my parents had gratefully accepted their invitation to meet at their home. It gave them the opportunity to see for themselves how the family lived. We were all a little apprehensive about the Vashi address. It was so far from town that it wasn't even considered to be in Mumbai, but Navi Mumbai or New Bombay, an altogether different city. For my thoroughbred townie parents, the only consolation was that I wouldn't be living there but in New York, post marriage. Apparently, we were all far more comfortable with an international calling code than a suburban postal code. It was absurd, I know. We paid the toll and crossed the bridge to Navi Mumbai with the kind of trepidation one usually reserves for entering a religious institution you don't belong to. And then, we felt like idiots. Their home was a beautiful two-storey bungalow in a quiet and leafy neighbourhood.

The meeting went off smoothly, although Maulik and I didn't actually 'meet'. He sat at one end of the room with his father, my father, his Mama and my Mama – yes, we'd both brought in extra troops – while I sat with the ladies.

His elder brother, Bhavesh bhai, the same one who'd convinced my mother to set up that first meeting, kept up a lively stream of chatter. Then, an hour later, when juicy topics for small talk were drying up and it seemed like everyone had sized everyone up, we took our leave.

'Nice family!' declared my father as soon as we were settled in the car.

'And nice house!' said my Mum.

'Good people, good people, indeed,' said Mama.

I smiled nervously and wondered if his family had felt the same way about us.

My phone beeped. It was Maulik.

'What's the good word?' he wanted to know.

I passed the phone around to everyone in the car, beaming. It was nice to finally meet someone who wasn't into the let-them-call-first game.

'Let's spend the day together tomorrow.' I typed back boldly.

'Sounds like a plan,' he said.

The day began pleasantly enough. I had gone to the salon for a professional blow-dry and had on a yellow jute dress with white hakoba flowers. I felt wonderful. We began with lunch at a nice Italian place and then moved to Kala Ghoda, the city's art district, to linger in some place over coffee. He had seemed quieter than usual that day, and we were on our second coffee when he finally opened up.

'Don't you feel this is all going too fast?'

I looked at him, surprised.

'I mean, we've only known each other for what … Five days? Isn't it scary?'

'I guess … but we have three months to…'

'I know, I know. But you know how it is, I'll go back to the US, get busy with work, you'll go back to your hectic routine, we will chat, maybe on the weekends. How much more will we really find out about each other?'

'Well, we can email and Skype and…' I fell quiet, unsure of where this conversation was really headed or of what was really bothering him.

'I mean, are we hurrying into this? How can we be so sure?' he said, staring gloomily into his coffee cup.

I looked at him uneasily. He had a point, I suppose. Three months of a fragmented long-distance conversation did not exactly qualify as a solid foundation for a happy married life. And yet, I couldn't share his apprehensions. It wasn't rational, my newfound serenity, but maybe I had just done this for so long that I could smell a good thing when I saw it in front of me.

'Let's take some time to think about it,' he said, as he dropped me home later that evening. 'We need a little distance.'

He was flying off to a different continent in a few days, wasn't that distance enough, I wanted to tell him. Couldn't we just keep meeting till then? But I didn't want to talk him into anything.

'Okay,' I said, 'talk soon.'

My parents were surprised to see me home earlier than usual.

'No dinner?' Mum asked.

I gave them a brief low-down of the day.

'But what could have gotten into him so suddenly?' my Dad wanted to know.

'Will they still be coming home on Saturday?' my Mum wondered.

While parting the night before, my parents had invited his family and him to visit us and they had already accepted. But now it seemed things might have changed.

'I don't know, guys,' I said. 'I have work tomorrow, I am off to bed.'

I felt bad for my parents. They tried not to show it, but I knew they were excited about the way things had been progressing. It was going to be a little devastating for them if this didn't work out after all. And yet, inexplicably, I remained unconcerned. The old me would've gone for a long, midnight swim in that vast sea of self-pity, but that night I picked up the copy of *Shantaram* lying on my bedside table and proceeded to read ahead.

Somewhere between sleep and wakefulness, it occurred to me that I had asked Manan to cut short his trip. It hadn't been the brightest idea to start with, but now it seemed absolutely ridiculous. If I called him now, I could still salvage his holiday. I sat up in bed and reached for my phone – but I couldn't bring myself to make the call.

The next day at work, Bhavesh bhai called me.

'What happened? Maulik won't tell us anything,' he wanted to know.

'Nothing. We're just taking some time to think about it, is all.'

'Well, think all you like. Just tell your parents we are still coming over on Saturday.'

They did come. Only, Maulik didn't.

'He has a deadline,' said Bhavesh bhai. 'He is working from home.'

My parents didn't know what to make of it all.

'Maybe his family is keen but he is not sure,' said my father after they'd left.

'But he seemed keen enough all this time,' said my Mum.

I refused to be drawn into their speculations. I was surprised that he hadn't come, and disappointed as well. But I was convinced that he wouldn't fly back to the US without at least speaking to me first. Turned out I was right. That night he texted to ask if we could meet the following day.

'Of course,' I wrote back instantly.

I could've been coy and said I would have to check with my parents, or taken my time to write back. But when you are going with your gut, there's no space for mind games.

'Hey, you know how we said we'd take the next few months to come to a decision?' he asked as soon as we'd picked a table and ordered our coffees. He looked much fresher and happier than when we'd met last. I nodded.

'Well, I don't want to wait that long.'

I stared at him.

'I want to get engaged before I leave,' he said. 'What do you think?'

I continued to look at him. I was surprised, but just for a moment, and not terribly so. It seemed natural to me that he should ask and that I should agree. Just like watching a movie that ends exactly the way you imagined it would. But this wasn't a movie, this was my life. I should've been terrified. I should've told him, 'That would be crazy! It's only been a week! Besides, why the sudden change of heart? What's gotten into you? How do I know you won't change your mind again?'

Instead, all I said was, 'Yes.'

A sure, unhesitating, uncomplicated 'yes'.

My answer caused quite a flutter at home. My parents had known that this final coffee date bode well, but they'd been content to sit back and wait out the three-month exploratory period we'd no doubt give ourselves. They not only expected me to take my time but also thought it advisable. But if I was convinced, they were happy. They'd waited for this day for a long time. They went about making the preparations for the engagement ceremony, to be held at our house the next day, with the excitement of little kids getting ready for a trip to Disneyland.

In the absence of any adult intervention in my supposed foolishness, my brother decided to don the mantle of the mature person in the family and plonked himself on my bed at night, while my parents were still making calls and inviting people to the ceremony.

'So you are really going to do this, huh?'

I nodded.

'It's only been a week, how can you be so sure?'

'I don't know ... I just am.'

Not convinced, he said, 'Okay ... don't worry, we'll just break it off later, if you feel you don't want to go ahead.'

'Okay,' I agreed, smiling.

'Okay,' he said, and having thus assured himself and me that this deal was retractable, he left the room.

Just then my phone rang.

'This had better be good,' growled the voice at the other end of the line.

'It is! It is!' I beamed into the phone.

It was Manan. He had rescheduled his flight and travelled overnight on the treacherous Delhi-Leh highway to come home early. And was I glad for whatever mad folly that had made me call him that day – I'd have hated for him to miss what was probably going to be one of the most important days of my life.

*

Maulik and I were engaged the next day in a small ceremony attended by close family and friends. He flew out that same evening. It is probably of no consequence but I remember thinking that day that the astrologers had got most of it right after all – I did marry outside my community, we did settle 8,000 miles away from home, and everyone agreed, it was all very sudden.

SOME HACKS ON HOW DOES ONE DECIDE

1. **Go with your gut – if you need to ask what that feels like, it's probably not a gut feeling.** This is not a decision that should be overthought. Yes, I am aware of how incredible that sounds, seeing as your entire life and happiness depend on it. But bear with me for a bit. This is an arranged marriage. What it lacks in matters of the heart cannot be compensated by reason. Before you even agree to that first meeting, the biodata has been analysed, due diligence has been conducted and the pros and cons have been weighed. And that is where all the cogitating should stop. After the coffees have been served and the initial jitteriness has been overcome, you need to stop evaluating whether you are right for each other and focus on

whether it *feels* right. Because it *can* happen. In this most contrived of settings, you can have the most natural of conversations. And that's the connection you should be looking for. No amount of thinking and rationalizing will get you there. You'll either 'click' or not.

2. **It's a life decision not a new haircut – you shouldn't have to be 'talked' into it.** The arranged marriage landscape is full of well-intentioned advice. Everybody in the know – and that pretty much means everyone you know – wants to help you make up your mind. It is easy to be influenced by a much-loved aunt, a grandparent, a best friend or even a respected family astrologer. But this, more than any other, is the time to drown out other voices and follow your heart.
3. **If you are not getting the feeling in a week, a month's not going to change anything.** I think the most bizarre advice you can get in the context of deciding if someone is right for you or not is 'give it time'. Why in the world would you want to give it time? It's not like it's a mouth sore that is going to get better with the passing of days. If there is absolutely no spark on your first date, what are you going to do differently on your second one? Carry a box of matchsticks?
4. **If you can't talk to them, it's a safe bet that you can't live with them.** Regardless of how awkward the arranged set-up is or how nervous he is or how

embarrassed you are – and regardless of how many times I've said it before – both of you need to be able to talk to each other. Not immediately, but yes, eventually. And it has to be good. Because if you can't swing a conversation, marriage is a long shot.

EPILOGUE

When I was in school, my friends and I used to play a card game called Fortune. Now, before I describe it any further, bear in mind that we studied in a strict Catholic high school. There were no boys and our only two male teachers were both 198 years old. We had no choice but to invent our own distractions.

Fortune involved two decks of playing cards, one of which was dealt out to the players, while the other was kept in a pile at the centre of the circle. Turn by turn, each player would have to make a prediction and pick a card from the common pile. The prediction would go something like this: 'Whoever gets this card will get a really romantic husband', or 'Whoever gets this card will have an extramarital affair'. Then the card would be upturned and we'd all check for identical cards in our own hands to see who amongst us was fated for home-cooked breakfasts in bed and who for clandestine hotel trysts. We had a wide range of predictions, from difficult mothers-in-law to the number of children to who'd settle abroad after marriage – every aspect of our married life was covered. But our most cherished prediction, which we made without fail and right at the beginning, was 'Whoever gets this card will have a love marriage'.

A love marriage was a very special thing in our heads. While little girls around the world dreamt of beautiful weddings, we Indian girls seemed to have taken a grand ceremony for granted. When we prayed to the Love Gods, we asked for a love marriage. Oh, how badly we wanted one. Maybe it was because all the beautiful people in the movies seemed to be having them. Or because it was what our cool cousin, the one who was gorgeous and who we wanted to be like, had after college. Or maybe because it was what our parents *didn't* have. I'm not even sure if we knew exactly why we wanted a love marriage, only that it was a terribly exciting thing.

A love marriage meant that you had a story. It meant that you'd been adventurous, that you'd been adored and wooed and pursued. You could gather your grandchildren around you some day and be sure to have their wide-eyed attention when you told them about how you met their grandfather. A love marriage made you interesting. As you can imagine then, my chief difficulty with having an arranged marriage was that it wasn't a love marriage.

And yet, now that I've been married for six years, I wouldn't pick one over the other. Not because love marriages have lost their glamour or arranged marriages have suddenly become cool, but because marriage, as I've learnt, is much more about the day-in-and-day-out business of living together, rather than how you got together in the first place.

When I observe couples around me, it seems that most marriages are varying combinations of pretty much the same things: love, companionship, sex, in-laws, children, chores, divvying up the chores, negotiations and arguments – arguments over who gets to pick the movie, who picks the restaurant and who picks the kids from craft class. There are mini fights and major fights, real apologies and pretend apologies. There are planned holidays, cancelled holidays and happy, happy holidays. There are expectations and disappointments. There is learning to live with the disappointments. There are kisses – goodnight kisses, goodbye kisses and a few (never enough) lingering kisses. And finally, there are lots and lots of meals – Sunday meals, hot meals, one-pot meals, three-course meals, meals that are eaten alone in front of the television, meals that are eaten together in front of the television, meals that are had in bitter silence, in bright conversation, over wine, over laughter. There are home-cooked meals and ordered-in meals and those wonderful meals that are followed by long, lazy naps.

In the end, it seems to me that it doesn't really – not

really, really – matter whether you met at a bar or at a coffee shop, whether your friends set you up or your parents, whether the love came before the marriage or after. The most important thing about a marriage is surely whether you enjoy being married to each other.

*

Some days when I am feeling exceptionally serene, like when the Universe has behaved itself and fallen in line with all of my heart's greatest desires – the baby has eaten and pooped in exactly the right quantities, my writing has come along swimmingly well, the husband has returned from work in time for dinner and all of the household help has decided to show up – on those days, I can actually look back at the husband-hunting days of my life and feel grateful for them. All those frustrating coffee 'dates' that came before that fateful afternoon when I met Maulik, taught me some pretty valuable life skills. I am listing a few below, perfectly aware that anyone who is currently doing the rounds of the arranged marriage circuit or even contemplating going on their first arranged 'date' is going to roll their eyes at this retrospective wisdom. But here it is anyway:

1. **You become a coveted dinner party guest.**

   I collected such an extensive repertoire of interesting anecdotes during my husband-hunting years that even if nothing funny were to ever happen to me again for the rest of my life, I'll never want for a dinner party invitation. Unless, of course, everyone at the said dinner table has read this book, in which case they will already know all my funny stories, and I will have to come up with new material. Which up until a year ago would've seemed like a daunting prospect, but now that I have a baby who farts so loudly that she scares herself and who thinks it is perfectly acceptable to howl and clap hands at the same time, I am sensing that a whole new source of funny may be making itself available to me.

2. **You develop a rare kind of perseverance.**
   There is really no other way you can spend Sunday after Sunday listening to forty men talk about how they spend their Saturdays.
3. **You can talk to anybody.**
   Nothing quite teaches you small talk like watching a bunch of people sitting awkwardly around a table, clinging desperately to the subject of the best barber at the Precious hair salon, lest they run out of things to say to each other.
4. **You become a good judge of character.**
   I am not sure how it happens or when exactly, but at some point when you've met, observed and spoken to enough new people, you learn to see through some of the bullshit.

5. You develop a sense of humour.

If you can't laugh about being set up with forty guys, how are you going to bring yourself to meet the forty-first?

ACKNOWLEDGEMENTS

Thank you Manan and Shilpi for your sun-like presence in my life. Without you guys, I'd have never made it through those hard husband-hunting years.

Thank you Diya Kar Hazra and Pranav Kumar Singh for your faith, support and guidance.

Thank you Sushmita Chatterjee for editing with sensitivity.

Thank you Mita Kapur for believing in the idea from the beginning.

Thank you to the entire team at Pan Macmillan India for making this story into a book. An actual, with its own just-off-the-press smell, book.

Thank you Deepti for all that precious, precious help and honesty.

Thank you Swati for all those nourishing conversations on writing, and to Shirin for always wanting to know how the book was coming along – sometimes that was all there was to keep me from giving up.

Thank you to all those friends and friends of friends who took time out to share their stories with me.

And finally, thank you to Mummy, my mother-in-law, if you hadn't offered to babysit every so often, I'd still be writing this book.